What others are saying (continued from the back cover)

"..., Fun ... Great information. Thanks so much for giving me the opportunity to dream a little about getting out of the city and building a small pond. One day soon..."

"A great 'homespun' alternative to the wildly expensive brochures, catalogues and garden centres out there."

"...love the economical attitude!!!!!!
That's what keeps the hobbies affordable and therefore a long lasting one."

".... the complete encyclopedia on pond building.
... very informative and the pictures and drawings were invaluable."

"..by far the most complete and detailed."

" WOW!! ... helping us not so creative minds feel like we can do this. "

"... definitely the envy of every pond site on the whole damn web!
No joking I mean it from the heart."

"At last, some one who understands that paying lots of money
may not get the job done!"

"... EXACTLY WHAT I WAS LOOKING FOR!!!!"

"... a great and informative source for beginners."

"... this is an excellent resource!"

"I did one out front, now I finally know all the people on my road after 18yrs.
They all stop to say hello."

"Informative and fun to read.
Also appeals to my sense of humour and economy."

".. the best source of pond information I have found ...."

"... appreciate the friendly tone and useful tips."

"... a great job describing in an understandable and interesting way."

"... The way it was written made my day. I am considering doing a pond but wasn't sure what all was involved. I couldn't believe here is was - do this and this and this. Thank you."

"... by far the most informative,"
"A great 'homespun' alternative to the wildly expensive

"...love the economical attitude!!!!!!
That's what keeps the hobbies affordable and therefore a long lasting one."

".... the complete encyclopedia on pond building.
... very informative and the pictures and drawings were invaluable."

"..by far the most complete and detailed."

" WOW!! ... helping us not so creative minds feel like we can do this. "

"... definitely the envy of every pond site on the whole damn web!
No joking I mean it from the heart."

"At last, some one who understands that paying lots of money may not get the job done!"

"... EXACTLY WHAT I WAS LOOKING FOR!!!!"

"... a great and informative source for beginners."

"... this is an excellent resource!"

"I did one out front, now I finally know all the people on my road after 18yrs.
They all stop to say hello."

"Informative and fun to read.
Also appeals to my sense of humour and economy."

".. the best source of pond information I have found …."

"… appreciate the friendly tone and useful tips."

"… a great job describing in an understandable and interesting way."

"… by far the most informative,"

"… it was the best … we have ever seen and we have seen a lot!"

"I give it better than Excellent, how about *WOW* "

"I have been thinking of putting in a pond but the cost has been choking me,
but no more."

"…a small pond in the back yard and have a little anxiety about being able
to keep it going. You've given me confidence!"

"This is the first … I have read about pond filters that I really understood."

"I did everything wrong the first time and in process of rebuilding,
I think I'll try three of your filters in a row!!"

"… brilliant. Now going to upgrade my filtration unit
(a commercially bought one) to encompass the ideas you have illustrated."

"…excellent technical advise and not a bad sense of humor ..."

"Finding (this) now will save us a lot of trial and error and money."

"… a lot of good stuff that don't require an arm and leg to do thanks"

"Very well scribed, practical, and knee-slappin' funny. "

(And there's a lot more but I'll save it for the next book)

THE

Ponder's Bible

by

G. H. Lovgren

First Edition

The Ponder's Bible

By Gösta H. Lovgren

With illustrations by Howard Bender

Published by:

Carolelle Publishing
12 Trenton Avenue
Lavallette, NJ 08735
1-800-409-0508

Copyright 1999   ISBN 1-929741-08-1

Library of Congress Card Number: 99-091385

First printing 1999   Printed in the United States of America

(A full color version of The Ponder's Bible is available.

See the coupon at the back of the book.)

From the Author

Hi, my name is Gösta H. Lovgren (most folks call me "Swede") and I have a backyard pond "page" on the Internet that is very popular and receives unfailingly "Excellent" reviews by the tens of thousands of visitors to it every year. I have decided to put what I have learned together in a book for you "non-netters" out there.

I'm a "do-it-yourself" kind of guy so this book is geared that way. This book is not intended for those who wish to establish acreage size ponds (Big "ponders" have a whole different set of problems and factors to contend with.) or can afford to hire a landscape architect at $25k plus. This is only for those folks who want a small piece of nature in the backyard without having to mortgage the kids. You can build a dandy looking pond with a dynamite filter system for under $500 (though you will likely go closer to $1,000) and only a few bucks a month to run.

> You should read this book all the way through before starting your pond project, then use it for reference as you are building. Leave yourself lots of lead time to noodle things over between the first reading and the start of the project. Ideas will be stimulated by your imagination and you can mull them over at odd moments.

It should be understood at the outset that if one talks to 100 "ponders" (Pond aficionados), It will result in at least 350 ideas on how to best build one. Mainly consisting of: "How I built this one (100)", "What I wish I had done (100)" and "My next one is gonna be like (150)".

Acknowledgements

I have to start with my wife, Carol-Lou, a school teacher (Teacher of the Year in 1992 I'm very proud to say), for her patience all these 35 years putting up with one hare brained project after another. Surely her background and training in dealing with little kids was a great help to her.

To Howard Bender for his help and patience with the illustrations in this book.

To my son, Keith, an author in his own right who encouraged me to write **_The Ponder's Bible_** in the first place. And then further encouraged me to start my own publishing company after the very frustrating process of finding a publisher. He also acted as critic, editor and proofreader. The relationship between editor and author is often a complex and difficult one. Keith handled it very well.

To the literally 1,000's of visitors to my pond site and take the time to write their appreciation. I owe them much.

And finally, the best for last. My son Kevin, about whom you will hear much in this book, for his unfailing good humor and untiring labor in bringing the old man's (sometimes nutty) ideas to fruition. Especially the failures (and there were/are many).

Table of Contents

Chapter Three – Waterfalls & Aeration   **63**

63

Chapter 1 Location & Excavation

Rules

First of all, there really aren't too many "rules" in pond making, and even those are often ignored. Essentially a pond is just a hole in the ground filled with water. The key is KEEPING the water in the hole instead of in the ground. Look around your yard for a likely location. My recommendation is to find a spot that is sunny all day. Most pond flowers require lots of sun. You have probably heard that sun will cause the pond to get "green with algae" and that certainly can be the case if you aren't planning to have a filter system. (Filters are discussed in Chapter Two.) Many folks have ponds with only a few fish and lots of plant life to act as "natural" filters. If that's the kind of pond you want, you would probably be better off if your pond only got sun a portion of the day.

If you have a deck or porch in your yard, having your pond right next to it, even as high as the deck level can be very attractive. Nothing sweeter than sitting on a shaded deck in the hot summer afternoons or evenings listening to a cool clear waterfall. No need to have a level surface either. Ponds can even be put in the side of a hill.

Try not to get too near trees if possible. Leaves have to fall somewhere and you likely don't want them in the pond. Then again, a nice shady tree to sit under in the hot of summer while daydreaming alongside the pond ain't too shabby either. If the pond will look good near or even under a tree, by all means locate it there. Try to make sure that at least a section of the pond will get a lot of sun though. If there is an extensive tree root structure to contend with, there's no rule that says the pond HAS to be below ground. *(more on that a little later on in this chapter)*

Make absolutely certain you are not digging in an area where electric, gas, water or septic lines are located. Not only is it dangerous (even if they are deep enough for the pond to sit on top of) should you ever have to get at them for maintenance and/or replacement years down the road, you will be in the soup if the pond is sitting on top of them.

Now you know the "rules" all you have left to do is decide what kind of pond you want. Essentially there are two kinds:

Pre-formed Ponds.

These are fiberglass pond shapes you can get at Home Depot, garden centers and large aquarium stores. They are the simplest to install and maintain. They often come as part of a kit that includes a filter and pump. Preformed ponds come in a myriad of shapes, sizes and configurations.

The main advantage to them is they are relatively simple to install. Once you have found your location essentially all you have to do is hollow out a shallow hole in the ground and plunk them down. Or you can just lay them on the ground and landscape around them.

The disadvantage is they are limited in size. They seldom hold more than 100 gallons of water and aren't very deep. Some plants require deeper water and dirt for their root systems than is possible with many/most preformed ponds. It's difficult to keep fish in them in the winter and all but the smallest fish tend to get very nervous in a shallow pond. Too close to potential predators I guess.

I do know of one fella who bought a huge stainless steel vat, something like a thousand gallons, at a dairy farm auction and is using that for his pond. {*Talk about a lifetime liner guarantee!*} I guess that comes under the heading of "preformed". Whatever holds water and works for you.

One good thing about pre-formed ponds is they can be a relatively simple starter pond and your investment won't have been "wasted". Later on it can be incorporated into a larger pond setup as a secondary or intermediate pond when you decide later on to go to a bigger setup. As you'll see, most all "ponders" do.

Form Your Own Ponds.

These come in two varieties, concrete or liner. The concrete type I'm sure you are familiar with. They are not projects for the average do-it-yourselfer however. The liner type is the pond we will be dealing with here.

When you have chosen the perfect location for the pond, it's time to lay it out. One nice thing about liners (there is a list of liner and other pond equipment sources in the References Chapter) is you can have your pond virtually any shape you want. Get a length of clothesline or a garden hose and use it to lay out various shapes on the ground.

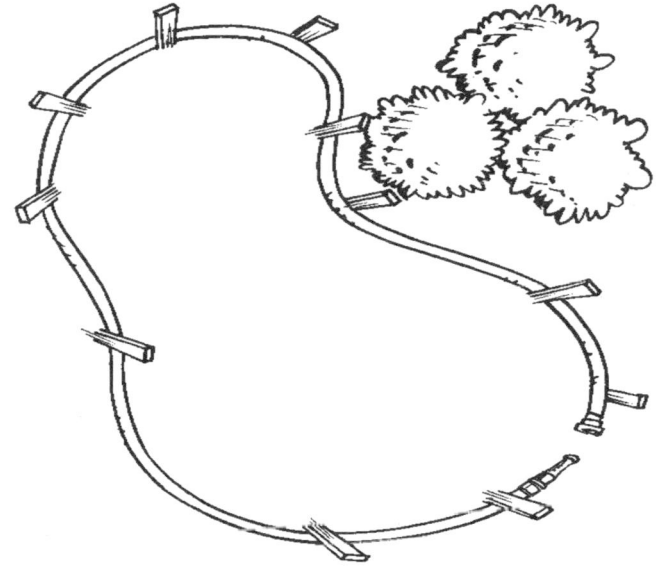

Once you have chosen the size and shape you want, now you can decide on the depth and what kind of sides you want on the pond. It's best to do this step on paper first. (You may want to make a sketch of your whole yard, shrubbery and all, to see how it all ties in.)

> You may find it easier to use spray paint to mark the outline on the ground rather than trying to keep the hose or clothesline in place when digging the hole.

Depth

There are no rules here but it should be deep enough so a section of the bottom is below the normal frost line in winter so the fish and plants won't freeze. In most areas of the US, 15" oughtta do it, but you will likely be better off going deeper. I would recommend 18-24" for a minimum but not over 36". If it's too deep, maintenance can be a problem, not that maintenance is going to be a chore but there are always things to do. The whole pond doesn't have to be that deep (15") but there should be a good size section that is anyway. It will provide a haven for your fish in the winter freezes.

Sides

For sides essentially there are three choices:

Straight sides - One advantage to straight sides is that it yields the most water volume capacity for the liner use. Generally the larger the water volume of a pond, the more stable it will be environmentally. For example a larger pond takes longer to warm up and takes longer to cool and is less stressful on pond life. Within broad limits it really doesn't take any longer or cost any more to maintain a larger volume as opposed to a smaller one.

Another advantage to straight sides is if you have raccoons near you (and almost everyone does these days), you don't have to worry about them eating your fish. They like to sit in shallow water and catch unsuspecting delicacies. Straight sides preclude that activity.

A disadvantage to straight sides is that it can make it difficult to get in and out of the pond to do maintenance. (If you become a true ponder you're going to want to get in there to move that plant or rock "just so", I promise you.)

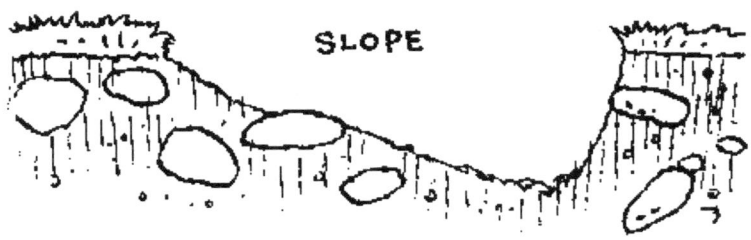

Sloped Sides - The advantage to vee and sloped sides is they provide a more "natural" look to the pond. I have a friend who laid large flat rocks on the slopes of his long (20'+), but narrow (6') pond so that it looks like a stream bottom. It's very impressive to look at. You don't HAVE to use flat rocks. 4-6" diameter "river stone" would look very good as well. (Or you don't need stone at all. It's your pond, you can have anything you want. Or nothing if you want.)

A minor advantage to sloped or vee sides is that it takes *slightly* less liner to get the same width. This could be a factor if you are working close with a standard liner size and/or want to tease out a little wider pond.

> You don't have to make your sides look just like the drawings (nor probably should you). They are just to give you a general idea.

Step Sides - Step sides have a "plant shelf", usually about 8-12" deep and 12" wide to hold plants along the edge. In my pond I have a "shelf" on one end with flat stones stacked on it. It provides a place with lots of nooks and crannies for the smaller fish to hide and frolic in.

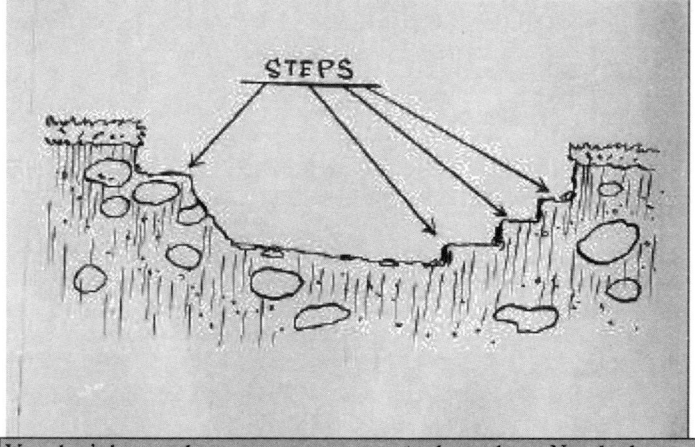

> You don't have to have as many steps as is shown here. Nor do the steps have to go all the way around the pond. This is just to show some possibilities. Nor do you need steps at all, but I recommend you put one in at one end at least.

A Step Side will use about the same amount of liner, or just a tad more, as straight sides. The step eliminates the need for plant holders or "tables". (If your pond is 18" or more deep, you may need something to bring the lilies and other plants to within about 12" of the surface for best flowering.)

If you decide to go with a Step Side(s), (and it isn't "necessary") be sure the shelf is pitched slightly towards the side. If you try to make it exactly level the shelf is likely to get pitched towards the pond as the liner conforms. This makes it difficult to get plants to stay on the shelf after slippery slime algae forms on the liner (and it will in a healthy pond).

There's no rule that says your pond must be on level ground either. It could be on a hillside. With a little imagination and a decent pressure pump (pumps are discussed in the next chapter) you could have a dandy stream running down the hill filling a series of ponds as it makes its way to the bottom. (*I'm getting ahead of myself a little here. We'll talk about streams in a later chapter. Talking ponds will do that to me. {sheepish grin}*)

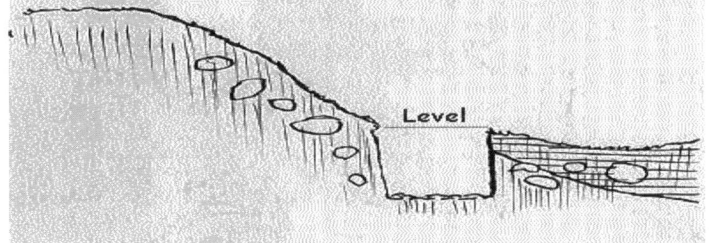

In this view, a hole is dug in the ground and the excavated dirt is used to build up one side enough to get a bank for the lower side of the pond.

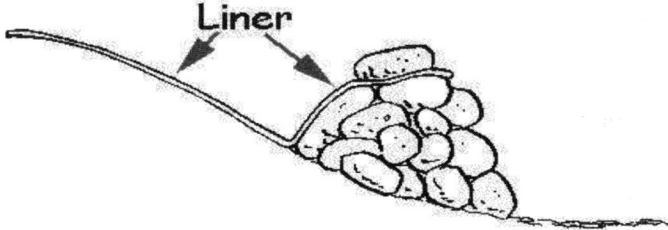

You can see how rocks are used to make a bank and how the liner is laid.

Measuring for liner size.

After you have determined the shape of the pond and the type sides you it will have you can then figure out what size liner to buy. (*Do this on paper first!!!*) Measure how many linear feet across it is across at the widest point and at the longest point. To each measurement add 2 times the deepest depth, then add 1' to each measurement for an edging overlap (trust me, you're gonna need it). Don't worry if you order more than you really think you will need. Most likely you will find other uses for the surplus liner, especially if you put in a waterfall.

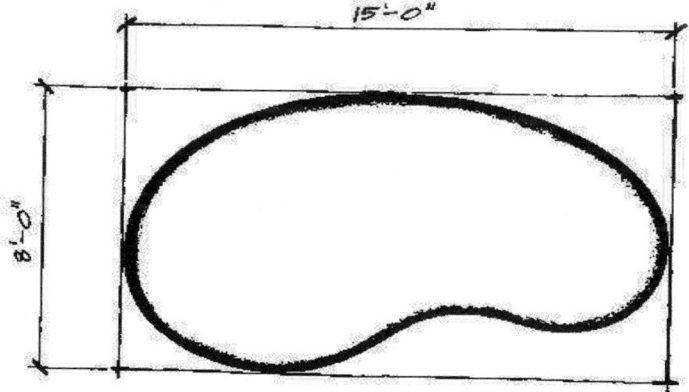

Example: Let's presume a pond that is 15' at its longest point and 8' at its widest point and is 24" deep at the deepest end. The size would be 15' (length) plus 4' (2' down for each side for the deepest depth) plus 2' (1' for edging on each end) which equals 21'. Then 8' (width) plus 4' (sides) plus 2' (edging) equal 14'. So you would need to order a liner at least 21' by 14'.

SECTION VIEW

Note- in this example as 21' is one foot over a "standard" liner size and there are sizable price jumps in liners over 20' long (wide), you may choose to adjust your pond size down a little and/or skimp on the edging a little. That's a decision you can make after talking to a liner supplier and comparing costs. You can glue liner together to make wider/longer measurements but gluing is not a trivial job for novices and I would advise against it. We (well my Kevin actually) did it, but it requires a patience and attention to detail that is beyond most people (or at least me, but not him).

Also when planning for the liner remember to allow for at least a 4"-6" deeper hole than your planned water depth to allow for a gravel and/or mud bottom.

Now that you have a rough size for your liner, you can go shopping. And it does pay to shop. Aquarium stores, home repair centers (Home Depot, etc.), garden centers, and places like that often carry (or can order) pond liners. There are specialty places just for pond liners as well (see References Chapter) which is probably your best bet. Another place to check with is roofing contractors. You just might get lucky and find one who has a large piece left from a job. It's pretty much the same stuff as pond liner. The only thing you have to watch for is that some roofing has an algaecide impregnated on one side and you have to make sure that side is not exposed to the pond if it does. Or maybe you know someone who is replacing their swimming pool liner or ....

Liner types - There are several different pond liner types but EPDM rubber is getting to be the standard these days. It's flexible to install, extremely temperature tolerant, and stands up very well to the elements (sun, snow, etc.). While 45 mil EPDM is the most common weight used for ponds, you may elect to spend a few bucks more and go for the 60 mil weight. This is especially true if you think you will be walking on it a lot or expect to share the pond with animals (dogs, raccoons etc.). EPDM is supposed to have a minimum life of 20 years which is pretty good in today's world of planned obsolescence.

Tetra (the fish food and aquarium products company - see References) makes a very durable vinyl liner as well though there isn't the availability of liners for really large ponds, say over 15'.

As a rule of thumb, you can expect to pay anywhere from 33 cents to $1.50 a square foot for EPDM liner, depending on a lot of factors like delivery, size, weight, etc. In the example above (15' x 8' pond) a liner should cost somewhere between $100 and $400. A pretty wide range I know, that's why it pays to shop around. (There are several liner sources listed in the References chapter.)

Digging the Hole

Now that you have the liner standing by you can dig the hole. Take the garden hose (or clothesline) and outline the shape when you have your shape figured out. There are no rules to pond shapes or sizes. Drive a wooden peg or stake every few feet next to the line to outline the hole in case the line shifts when you are digging.

> Don't dig the hole ahead of time. More than one would-be ponder has done that and had a heavy rain before the liner got delivered. A real mess and a lot of extra work then.

If you are digging in sandy soil and the banks or sides keep caving in before you get a chance to get the liner laid, what you can try is filling bags (those ubiquitous plastic shopping bags we all have so many of laying around) with dirt and laying on the sides of the bank. Or some old carpeting. Or ... Anything to keep the dirt from moving until you can get the liner down and the weight of the water on it.

You have to get rid of the dirt you are taking out. If the place you are putting the pond is a low lying area that gets flooded in a decent rain or is subject to runoff, you should use (some of) the excavated dirt to build an embankment around the pond. The banks will keep runoff (which may contain mud or may be contaminated with fertilizers, weed killers, etc.) from getting in the pond.

Another advantage to an embankment is you don't have to dig as deep. Though if you are the foreman (as I always try to be) that may not be as much a consideration.

> If you decide to elevate the ground around the pond, make sure the top of the embankment is at least 18-24" wide and is level. If you have a sloping or narrow top, the embankment t will be uncomfortable to stand on to look in the pond.

Other uses for the excavated dirt could be as a base to fashion a stream bed from your filter location back to the pond. Or as a base to sit your filter on behind your 20' high waterfall.

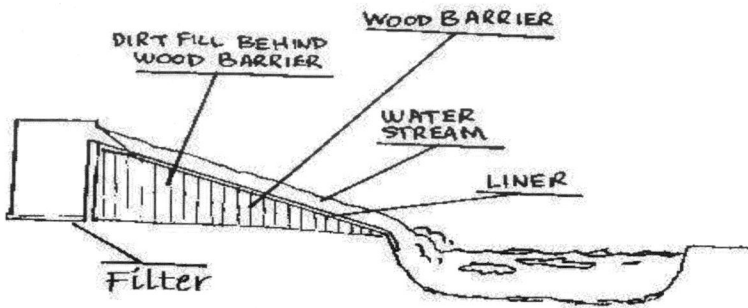

Don't forget to allow for several inches for gravel and padding depth when digging. If you plan on gravel bottom, or even a section for a mud bottom, you must make it that much deeper. (If you want a 24" deep pond, dig to about 30" deep.) As you will see in the Plants Chapter, you may even want to have one end (or section) that has a 6 to 12" deep "mud hole" covered with gravel so you'll have to plan for that as well.

Keeping it Level

It's critical at this point to maintain a level plane all around the edges of the pond. You can do it with a long straight board and a carpenter's level.

Pond Supplies of America (see References Chapter) sells a nifty little gadget that attaches to each end of a garden hose that fills with water to determine a level over long distances. Better yet you could make your own level by taping a clear plastic soda bottle (with the bottom cut off) on each end of a garden hose. Another trick is to take a long length of clear tubing and fill it with colored water (*actually the guy I saw used wine but ...*). No matter what method you use, be very careful, even anal, about the leveling technique. If the pond sides aren't level now, it will be almost impossible to correct later on and will look terrible if it's grossly out of level.

Around the top edge of the hole, dig back a "shelf" about an inch or two deep and 12-24" wide. This is where the edging overlap of the liner will go and be covered with stones, grass, or something else to hide the liner edges. As you can see in the illustration the liner extends out past the edge of the pond and is covered with turf on one side and stone on the other.

If you are planning to have something heavy abutting the pond (like a rock waterfall), you should put some wooden shoring along that edge between the liner and the ground.

Otherwise the weight of the waterfall stone may eventually, even likely, cause the sides of the pond liner to bulge into the pond or even fail. 1" X 6" treated lumber will work nicely. The illustration shows the wooden shoring but the liner actually covers it.

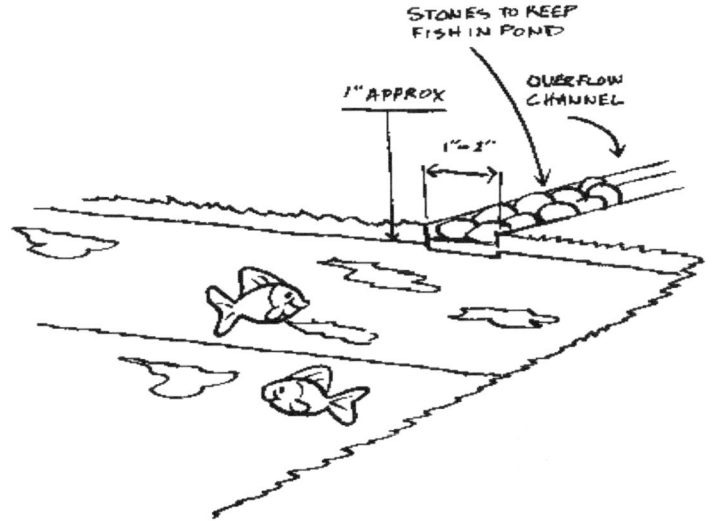

In one place you may want to have a small section, maybe a few inches wide, that is a little lower than the rest (an inch is more than plenty). This is to control overflow from heavy rain. You can fill it with stones to keep fish from escaping during high water events.

The illustration shows an elaborate overflow channel. You likely wouldn't need anything this fancy unless you had a continually fed source of water from a spring or something like that. Or the pond was subject to sudden large water charges, say from heavy rainfall channeling into it.

Setting the Liner

Before setting the liner, you should line the bottom with a buffer material. *Clear out any sharp stones or anything that might possibly puncture the liner first.* An inch or two thickness of newspapers work very well. Even better if you can find some old carpeting. It provides a protective buffer between the weight of the water on the liner and any rocks that may make their way to the surface from deep under the ground (natural phenomena that happen in many areas of the country). You could line the sides as well but they are not nearly as important as the bottom to line.

Next lay out the liner across the hole. This step will likely need two or three people (or a Kevin). The liner is very heavy and will require a lot of tugging and adjusting. In your bare feet, get in the hole and walk around the liner being careful not to pull on it so much that it tears. It's pretty rugged but no sense taking chances. Try to smooth out the wrinkles on the bottom and sides. Don't try to get too fussy though. You really won't notice the wrinkles later. In the corners, fold and tuck the excess as best you can. Again, don't get too fussy. They really won't be very noticeable once the water is in and the algae grows a coat on the liner.

If you are going to have flat rocks on sloping sides you may want to put them in now. If you do, make sure to leave plenty slack in the liner for settling. It's probably a good idea to fill the pond first to get the liner to conform, then pump the water out and place the rocks. Or you can get in the pond and place the rocks after the pond has been filled. Or ...

After the liner is set in place, you can start filling it. The weight of the water will force the liner to conform to the shape of the hole so make sure you have plenty of slack all around the top. You may not need it but it's awfully hard to correct later if you don't have it.

Let the pond fill to the top, even overflow. That way you can check for level. If it's not level, now is the time to correct it. Pump the water out and make whatever adjustments are necessary or possible (*all the time cussing yourself for not being more anal when leveling in the first place*).

Now you can landscape the edges, laying the liner in the edging shelf and covering it with stones or grass or whatever.

Above Ground Pond

It's not absolutely necessary for the pond to be in the ground. You can make a very attractive above ground pond as well.

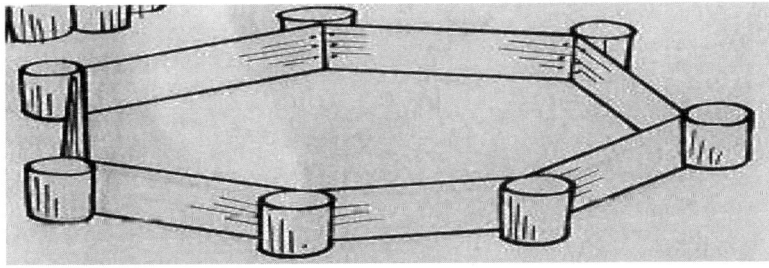

The illustrations show two possibilities for using cut off pilings (or tree logs or ...). If you decide to build something like the second one (with fewer pilings and filling in the gaps with wood, be sure to use at least ¾" plywood (or equivalent) if the gaps between the pilings are going to be greater than 18". There is a surprising amount of water pressure on the sides. Probably better to use 1" thick treated decking for the sides instead of plywood. Look better too. If the pilings are touching each other, it probably won't be necessary to fill in the gaps between them as the liner should be plenty strong enough to withstand the pressure over such a short distance.

(Courtesy of Terry Emyard)

It isn't necessary to use pilings, you could make a very nice enclosure using 2X4 framing (just like house framing) and covering the outside with shingles or some such. The same leveling rules apply here as well.

(Terry's pond finished)

If making a wall that will have a cap, then don't put the cap on until after the liner is installed. Drape the liner over the top of the wall and then fasten the cap.

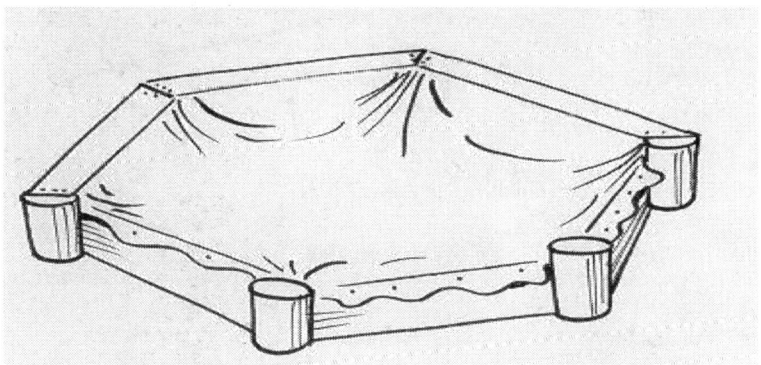

If you decide on an above ground pond, I don't think I'd make it much more than 18" to 24" high. *You'll probably start getting into wall support and bracing factors above that.* Besides 18" is a nice height to use as a bench to sit on while daydreaming. (Did I mention ponds are great for daydream inducement?)

Gravel Bottom

In the bottom of the pond put white gravel (I recommend 3-4" deep). You can use any grade of gravel or even stone but generally the finer the better. If you use a larger size (say ½ or bigger grade), look for smooth sided gravel as opposed to the sharp edged kind. A lot less likely to poke a hole in the liner if a heavy weight is sitting on it (like a flower pot or a boulder or big lunk walking around on it making "adjustments", or ...).

While many very nice looking ponds and apparently healthy ponds just have a bare liner bottom, I believe gravel is a necessity. Gravel is very healthy for a pond. It does all these things:

1. It vastly increases the surface area for bacteria to grow on that break down fish wastes, water discoloring algae, and other organic matter.

2. It provides a base for microscopic pond life to root in.

3. It gives the fish something to root in for food (algae).

4. It provides a light background to look into (if you use white gravel) - You'll be able to see the fish and other stuff a lot better. It's amazing the difference white gravel makes when looking down into it.

5. It spreads weight over a far larger area of the liner when walking on it. It also provides a large measure of protection from the sharp claws of any animals that may get into the pond.

6. The organic detritus that falls to the bottom of the pond (leaves, fish waste, etc.) will decompose much more rapidly due to the bacteria already growing in the gravel. A professional pond installer claims it's the difference between nothing and more than a foot of mulm to clean out every spring.

7. A surprising number of people have trouble with storks, egrets and great herons using their ponds as a local cafeteria, feeding on their beloved fish. The combination of white gravel and clear water make the depth of the pond difficult for them to gauge and as a consequence they won't land.

8. It gives a much more interesting and natural appearance to the bottom of the pond.

9. It provides an almost cost free opportunity for even more filtration. *(See the UG filter in the next chapter)*

One very important thing to remember is to wash the gravel thoroughly before putting it in the pond, *especially if adding to an already established pond.* It's likely covered with a very fine powder inevitably created from the stones rubbing together. When the powder gets suspended in the water it is so fine it will clog the gills of fish and even kill some plants. And the dust is so light it can take days/weeks to settle out. Thorough washing of any gravel is in order before putting any fish in the pond. One *relatively* easy way to wash gravel when adding it to a *new* pond is to put the gravel in the pond, cover it with maybe 6 inches of water, get in and stir the gravel around using an "upside down" rake.

Let the filling hose run in one end and have a pump working at the other. (Don't worry if the discharge turns the grass white, it will wash off with the next heavy rain.) Keep flushing until the water looks clear.

Measuring Pond Volume

This would be a good time to estimate how much water your pond holds. The formula is Volume (in cubic feet) times 7.5 (gallons in a cubic foot). To get the Volume, multiply the Length of the pond by its Width times its Depth. (Volume = Length X Width X Depth X 7.5). In our example the pond was 15' long by 8' wide and 24" deep so the formula is Volume = 15 X 8 X 2 X 7.5 = 1800 gallons. Now if you had sloping sides or an irregular shape it would be something less than 1800 gallons (conceivably as little as 900 gallons if the sides made a perfect V in a rectangular shape). At any rate now you have a *reasonable estimate* of what your pond holds. It's not critical to get an exact measurement, just an estimate.

Another way to measure volume is to measure how long it takes to fill a gallon jug (or 5 gallon pail) with your filling hose and then time how long it takes to fill the pond. If it takes 5 seconds to fill a gallon jug (12 gallons a minute) and two hours to fill the pond then you have a 1500 gallon pond. (*It actually works out to 1440 gallons but after all this work we're entitled to a little inflation, aren't we? Besides 1500 is an easier number to remember.*)

You will need the rough approximation of the gallon capacity to size for the filter and pump in the next chapter. You will need it for pond discussions too. You're going to have quite a few of them in the coming years. It doesn't have to be an exact figure. In the ballpark, close enough for government work, ... We're not talking rocket science or brain surgery here or filling out the 1040 long form.

Chapter 2 – Pumps & Filters

What used to be a serious esthetic problem was "green" water caused by a high algae growth (actually microscopic phytoplankton) usually precipitated and fed by fish wastes or other organics, and sunlight. There are innumerable kinds of algae but we are only concerned here with the kind that turns the water green. Dreaded Green water doesn't have to be a problem with the filter technology available today. It's not at all difficult to maintain crystal clear water.

Sparkling water secrets

There are two secrets to sparkling water:

One is a large, even over-capacity, biological and mechanical filtering system.

The second is easy cleaning and maintenance of the filter system. If the cleaning is easy and quick it will get done more often and more readily. If cleaning and/or maintenance are onerous and/or time-consuming (say an hour or more to do) it will inevitably be put off, which usually results in taking even more time or work. If it's a snap to do, it will get done in a timely fashion. The "ease of use" factor holds true for a lot more things than just filters too.

The lava rock filters described in this chapter fit those criteria (high capacity and low workload).

It's important here to remember one rule - **The filter(s) can only be too small, not too big**. If you don't mind green or cloudy water, and only want a few fish, or want to spend an inordinate amount of time cleaning filters, you can ignore this rule. Generally the more filtration, the more life your pond can support. If your pond is in full and direct sunlight (mine is in summer) it will have a lot of algae potential and become nearly opaque without a decent filtering system.

The 3 basic kinds of filtration

Essentially filtration boils down to three kinds:

1.Mechanical - which physically removes particulate matter from the water (but not algae). The drawback with mechanical only filters is they don't rid the water of the ammonia and other stuff from fish waste the algae feed on, so you can still get green water.

2.Biological – providing surface area for bacteria to grow on which break down matter (particularly ammonia from fish exhalation and excrement) into stuff that can be utilized elsewhere. Or uses plants to "amortize" the nutrients before the algae can (a "veggie" filter).

3.Chemical - Adding chemicals to the water to kill the *unwanted* algae, or in some way alter the water so the algae doesn't grow. I don't like and don't use chemical means in my pond.

Under "chemical", I would also put UltraViolet light, even though it's not strictly chemical. Water passes in front of UV tubes and the algae are killed. *There is one big advantage to UV light that is not minor* - It kills pathogens that infect fish. An important consideration if you have valuable fish (show quality koi for example). In either case (chemical or UV) the water discoloring algae is eliminated. My reasoning is that if it kills algae, what else does it kill as well? Dyed water (discussed later) also comes under the heading of "chemical" as well.

These explanations are simplistic but functional enough for this discussion. Effectively, in my pond I use the first two and religiously avoid the third.

> One other thing, when I'm talking about algae in this book, unless specifically stated otherwise I will mean the water borne kind that discolors the water (microscopic phytoplankton), the kind that biological filters take care of. There are all kinds of algae and the kind that grows on surfaces is generally healthy, if sometimes unsightly, for the pond and provides food for the fish.

Lava Rock Filter System

The absolute best simplest filter I have found after spending major league time and money experimenting is a lava rock system. (*This isn't to say other type filters don't work as well, they do. There are some good commercial filters on the market that do a very good job. Bubble beads and brushes to name just two examples. However they are often more complex, require more maintenance and are a good deal more expensive.*) My water stays sparkling clear (finally) with a heavy fish load, and my pond receives full sun all day in the summer.

Lava rock is extremely porous. It's so light that some pieces often float until they soak up water enough to sink. All that (interior) surface area will get covered with good bacteria that break down the ammonia from fish waste and eat the "food" that supports the algae that color the water green. Or more accurately removes the nutrients that algae thrive on. Further it makes a pretty fair mechanical filter as well but that's not its primary function.

One simple way is to make a large lava rock filter is out of a plastic 55 gallon drum. It's pretty easy. Here's how: Cut out the top the drum so it is open.

> Note - Cut inside the ring on the top of the barrel rather than underneath it on the side. The ring gives the barrel strength and rigidity.

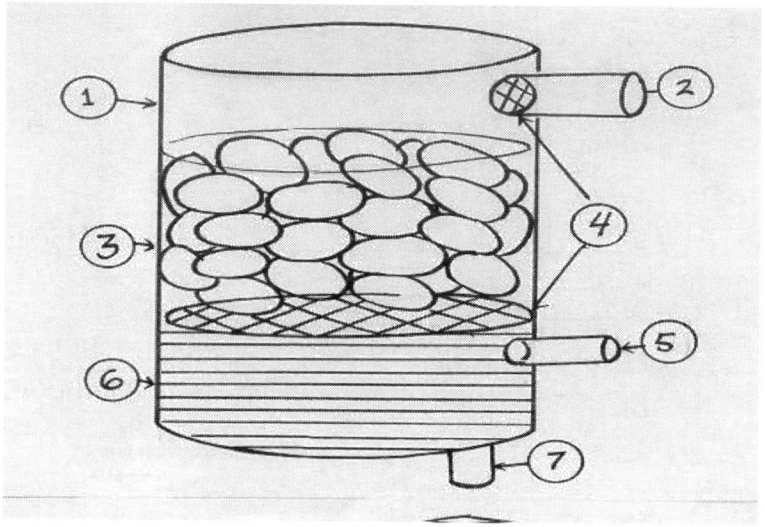

(1)

The floc water settlement area ("*Floc*" *is matter created by the bacteria, analogous to feces*), should be at least 2" between the bottom of the discharge pipe and the top of the lava to keep the floc from going into the pond. It could be a lot more but not less.

Cover the top of the lava rock with some sort of filter pad (*see References Chapter for filter padding sources*) so the floc gets caught in it and doesn't get discharged into the pond.

(2)

The discharge pipe(s), must be considerably larger than the input pipe. The water is coming in under pressure (greater than gravity) and is leaving under gravity. (*see AIR LOCKs in the Miscellaneous chapter as well.*) You don't need pipes, you could just as easily cut a slot in the barrel here if you wanted. Cut the hole about 2" high and 8" wide at top of the barrel. Again - don't cut the very top supporting ring though or you will weaken the barrel.

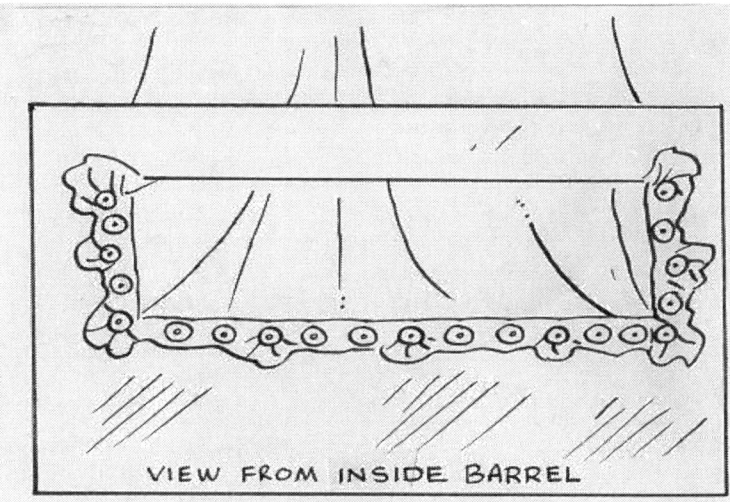

VIEW FROM INSIDE BARREL

Using a 12" wide by 24" long (or even longer) piece of liner, fasten one 12" end all around the hole on the *inside* with small screws and silicone the edge liberally. Then pull the other end through the hole and it will form a chute for the water to come out. Trim the "chute" to whatever length you think appropriate. (Note the "chute" idea isn't just limited to barrels, it can be used in almost any type filter container.)

(3)
The area filled with lava rock . The deeper this is the better, about a third or more of the barrel. You'll probably need 3 or 4 cubic feet. Better to have too much than too little.

(Note - while barbecue lava rock works well it's relatively expensive to buy in small bags. It probably costs 3 times as much that way. Also the bigger the chunks of lava rock the easier to flush clean in the filter (but less mechanical filtering it will do). If you have a choice when buying it in different grades the best size is would be in the 1" to 1½" grade area rather than the smaller pea gravel sizes.)

(4)

The egg crate grate *(see the Miscellaneous chapter for more info on egg crate)* the lava rock sits on. Also there is a small piece of grate in front of the discharge pipes in case some floatable plugs it up. *(Once my pond emptied when a piece of lava floated up and plugged one and the filter overflowed).*

You can sit the grate on top of a milk crate. Cut the milk crate down a little so the grate doesn't sit so high up in the barrel. Or you could use bricks to hold it up. Or … You only need about 2" or 3" clearance from the bottom. Just enough for the water input. That way there will be more room for lava rock should you think later on you need it.

(5)

The input pipe from the pond. This should be 1¼" as well, even if you are using a smaller pump. Under 1500 gph you can get by with 1", but if you ever want to go to a bigger pump you'll be sorry if you restrict it here. Make sure you locate the input JUST BELOW the grate the lava sits on.

(6)

The settlement area for dirt. Mine is about a third or a little less of the barrel. This height is not critical but shouldn't be more than a third of the barrel. The primary function this area serves is to allow the water to find its way evenly up through all the lava rock. It really doesn't need to be more than 2 or 3" high. Secondary is to allow room to flush the dirt into when cleaning. Contrary to accepted conventional wisdom there will be very little dirt settlement here. The volume of water coming into such a confined area will keep any sediment stirred up pretty good.

(7)

The clean-out drain. Mine is1¼". **DO NOT DO NOT DO NOT** *(a "rule")* use less than 1¼" here, even if you are using a smaller barrel or bucket. Filter flushing is just SO MUCH EASIER, FASTER AND BETTER with a large discharge it is a foolish economy to use anything smaller.

When the drum is filled with water put a filter pad (see References Chapter for padding sources) on top to catch the floc for even finer filtration, and/or put water hyacinth or something else fast growing on top of the rock. The roots provide additional filtering and the plants make a nice cover.

You don't have to use a barrel either. You can adapt almost anything to make a biological filter. One fella I know has a kiddy pool adapted to a filter using the same principles, with the top full of water hyacinth to cover it. Another I know replaced the sand in a swimming pool filter with lava rock and is using that.

If you have a smaller pond, say under 500 gallons, a five gallon bucket using the same principles should work nicely.

(My first *successful* barrel filter.)

Notice the large drain hose leading from under the bottom of it. The plant growing on top is called *water cabbage.* The input piping runs along the ground and into the other side of the barrel alongside the fence.

Plywood Filter

You can make a nice looking filter with plywood that will maybe fit into your decor better than an ugly old barrel. Maybe even cover it with siding to match the house. A single 4'x 8' sheet of ¾" plywood (*don't use less than ¾' wood for a span over 15-18", the sides will bulge out otherwise*) is all you need to make a BIG filter. Don't worry if the filter is "oversized". Remember it can only be too small.

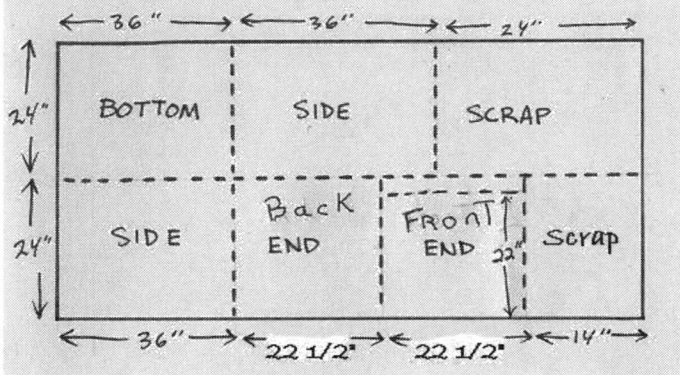

Notice the board marked "Front End" is only 22" high when the Back End is 24". That's where the water will discharge. All you have to do is make a chute out of the scrap pieces and fasten it to the front end after the filter box is assembled.

You can likely go to a home center and have the ¾" plywood pre-cut for you. Have it cut to the dimensions in the diagram and it will fit nicely together and make a filter housing big enough to easily hold more than 6-8 cubic feet of lava rock. (plenty big enough for a 3,000 gallon pond or even bigger).

To seal the plywood, you can fiberglass all the seams and surfaces inside. Make sure you get a good thick coat of resin on the inside walls, else the water will penetrate the layers of plywood and eventually weaken it (or leak). Glass the outside corners too for added strength.

But it would be a lot easier to just stick a piece of liner in there. It might even be cheaper to use liner by the time you get finished. You would need piece of liner 6' x 7'. If you decide to use liner, use 2x2's on all the inside corners to screw the plywood to.

Stock Tank instead of a barrel

(Picture courtesy of Trey and Jacque's Pond Page.)

It isn't necessary to use a barrel. Quite a few people have used "stock tanks" (a heavy plastic oval shaped open container used for feeding livestock). Above is a picture of a 75 gallon stock tank that has been covered with cedar or knotty pine to hide it.

(Courtesy of JBU8047150@AOL.Com)

A picture of a lava rock filter housing made from landscape logs and lined with EPDM liner. This is a BIG filter, at least 4' by 12' and 3' high. The owner claims he only has to flush it once a season and you can see how clear his water stays.

This was also a very attractive way to hide the filter.

The 16 gauge stainless steel filter in my own pond. It is the same dimensions as the plywood filter shown earlier. (That's how I know about the fiberglass leaking and the sides bowing. I built two of them before having this one built. {sigh}) *Notice the drain hose coming from the bottom and tied to the fence. Just have to let the hose fall and the filter drains right out. Couldn't be easier!.*

Notice too the water input is straight into the bottom of the filter. By piping directly into the filter with no elbows, I was able to increase *significantly* the amount of water coming from the pump. (We'll be talking more about piping a little later in the chapter.)

This is the discharge chute from my stainless steel filter. It's nearly 3' wide even though the filter is only 2' wide. The chute was made with one side 12" long and the other 36" to give a better view of the waterfall from the end of the pond. (It doesn't look it but there is over 100,000 gallons of water per day falling off the chute. **Now that's aeration, baby!**)

All these filters were built using the same principles as the barrel filter. Water percolating up through the lava rock and out a discharge at the top.

Depth of Lava Rock

However you make your filter (barrel, plywood or other), don't put the lava rock too deep as it will be harder to flush. Somewhere between 6-12" should work well. If it's shallower than 6" deep, it will still work fine as a biological filter (as long as there is enough rock capacity for the load being filtered – 1 cubic foot per 500 gallons) but it won't filter particulates as well. If it's greater than 12" deep, it will filter very well both biologically and mechanically (particulates) but it will be more difficult to flush well.

Pump Size

There you go, the filter is done. Use as large a pump as is practical. A rule of thumb I use is to have a pump large enough turn the pond over at least once an hour, more if possible. This is NOT cast in stone either. You could always start with a much smaller pump. It's been my experience that a great flow is not needed for the bacterial part of the filtration. It is nice to have a large flow for a waterfall though (waterfalls are in the next chapter) and circulation (aeration) in the pond.

Filter cleaning

All it takes to clean the filter is to shut the pump off, drop the drain hose on the filter and drain it.

It helps if you have a garden area nearby to drain into. Nutrient rich water and a lot of good "garden material" will be getting flushed out every week or so. No sense letting it go to waste. You can even use a long drain hose if your garden area is far away from the filter as long as the bottom of the filter is higher than the area you want to "feed".

Take a garden hose turned on full <u>but without the nozzle</u> (*we want volume, not pressure*) and start flushing the filter right through the top of the filter pad. (If you use a filter pad on top of the lava rock, and I recommend you do.) You can take the pad out and flush it separately if you want but be careful. It will be very heavy with water and can tear easily. Keep flushing until you don't see any more dirt chunks or discolored water coming out of the drain hose.

The Ponder's Bible

I usually clean mine about every 10 days or two weeks during the summer when the water is warm and the fish are most active. It only takes 5 or 10 minutes. The secret is the large 1¼" drain on the bottom. You'd be surprised how much longer a 1" drain takes, never mind a ½.

> The pond may get a cloudy or "dusty" look for a few hours after flushing the filter. Not to worry. That's just fine particulate that has been disturbed and will clear up quickly.

Cleaning note - Lift the filter pad off every once in a while, say once a week. If you see the water "channeling" up through the lava in places, you can be pretty sure it's starting to get plugged. Channeling is serious and means the area of lava rock exposed to the moving water has been drastically reduced, seriously reducing biological efficiency. Don't put off cleaning it if it channels. It isn't working well and will only plug harder making it more difficult to flush.

Be sure to flush the lava rock thoroughly to prevent dirt buildup in spots. If channeling happens frequently, even after thorough flushings, it means a dirt buildup within the body of the filter has occurred that is significantly compromising the lava rock. You will then have to take the lava rock out to flush it properly. Flush every week or so in the summer (heaviest load months) and channeling should never be a problem or you.

When first starting up the lava rock filter, flush it every couple of days for the first week or two, especially if the pond was turbid or murky to begin with. It will be picking up an abnormal amount of particulate and there's no sense giving it a chance to plug the lava rock before it even can establish a bacteria colony.

A murky pond will start to clear almost immediately for the first few days, maybe even to the point of being able to see the bottom, as a result of the filter taking out particulates. What will often happen then is the pond will cloud up again (*though not as bad as before*). Don't worry if that happens. The bacteria have yet to get fully established and the sun has penetrated to a greater depth in the clearer water, allowing yet more algae to bloom. The clear/cloudy cycle may occur several times in an already established pond or even a new one. As soon as enough bacteria get established it will clear up better than ever and stay clear.

Bacteria colonies will begin to form by themselves in as little as two weeks if the water is warm (70+F) and well oxygenated. It can take much longer if the water is cold and won't even get started until the water gets above 45-50F degrees. There are bacteria "starter" kits on the market but I have never used them. Essentially all they do is cut the time it takes for the filter to get established by a few days/weeks.

Another important advantage to lava rock is that flushing doesn't wash away the bacteria colony like it does on the brush, bubble or even filter mat type filters. Bacteria only grow and propagate on surface areas and with those type filters it gets easily washed off when exposed to a high water flow. Whereas with lava rock, the vast bulk of the bacteria is on the interior of the rock and won't get washed off by high water flow. This virtue allows it to work in high flow conditions. The pump size can be increased without the loss of bacteriological efficiency such as usually happens with other filter material.

Undergravel Filters

When building the pond, you should seriously consider putting in undergravel filters. They are absurdly cheap and easy to install in the pond construction phase. Essentially they are undergravel filters just like those used in aquariums. Take 2 (or 1 or 3 or ...) pond lengths of 1" to 1 1/2" PVC pipe (or you can use that black plastic irrigation tubing and save a few bucks here too) and drill them full of 3/8" holes (any size actually but if they are too small they may eventually get plugged with grass algae) about 6" apart and lay them on the pond bottom.

Drill the holes so that the most of them will be on the sides of the pipes instead of the tops when they lay on the bottom. They'll be less likely to have the weight of the gravel plugging them up that way. No big deal, but as long as you're doing it you might as well give yourself the best advantage.

Put an elbow on one end pointing up and a piece of pipe long enough to be about 6" below the water surface when the pond is full. Plug the other end with a pipe cap. (Note there is no need to use glue for the joints. There's no pressure involved and we don't care if they "leak").

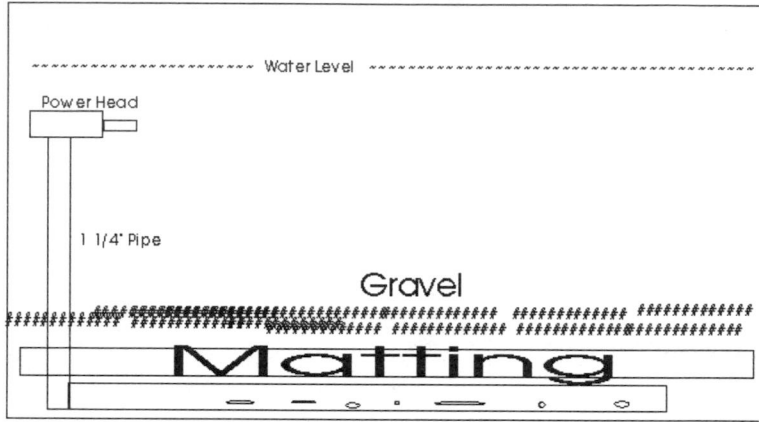

Lay synthetic matting (see References Chapter) on top of the pipes and the gravel on top of the matting. I prefer matting because it adds just that much more area for bacteria to grow, but not a big deal though if you use something else.

You could even use plastic or nylon window screening on top of a more rigid plastic mesh (just not a metal that will eventually rust or corrode). The reason for the rigid mesh is that you don't want the screening (or matting) to wrap around the pipe when you put the gravel on top. It's okay if it "tents" over the pipe, just so it doesn't wrap tightly. The object is to increase the "draw" area as much as possible.

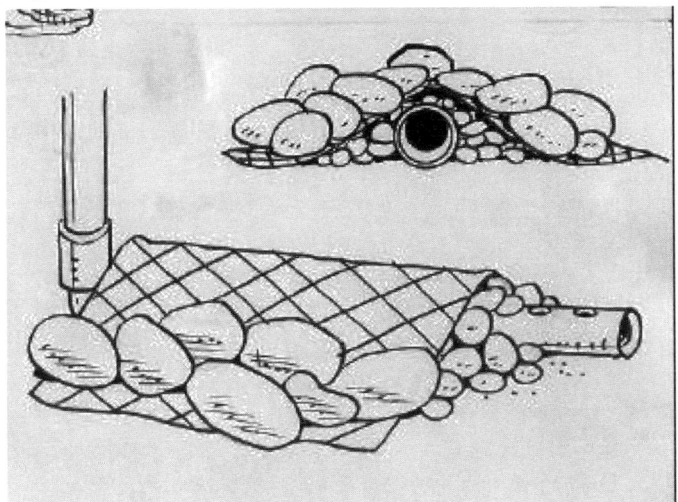

If you don't have a rigid mesh to prevent the matting or screening from wrapping around the pipe, you could always lay large stones alongside the pipe and lay the matting (or screening) to prevent wrapping to tightly. If a section of the pipe will be laying on a mud section, you may want to put a strip of plastic 3 or 4" wide (like a garbage bag) under the pipe, so it won't draw the mud up into the pipe.

From your local aquarium store, pick up a "power head" (a small aquarium pump) for each pipe. I got mine mail order from That Fish Place for $17 apiece (see References Chapter). 300 gph each (NOT larger - you don't want too much suction through the gravel). Power heads will fit nicely on top and inside of 1" & 1¼" pipes. I have my pipes cut so the tops of the pumps are 2 or 3 inches below the surface. They provide an almost imperceptible surface current greatly increasing the oxygen interface exchange and work as an ice deterrent in the winter.

UGs are cheap and easy to put in (even if unnecessary overkill) so why not do it? If you stick the pipes in when you're building the pond, it's almost no additional work. You can add the pumps anytime.

You could even use aquarium airstones instead of power heads to pump the water as well (even be cheaper to run and would provide even further aeration).

I'm really pleased with mine and strongly recommend them to anybody building a new pond. They are so easy to make and very cheap to run (30 watts per pump - maybe $1.50 a month for electricity), it's almost a crime not to install them. I let mine run all winter (moving water normally won't freeze) even after I have to shut the waterfall off (ice). Even when the surface does freeze, it thaws quickly as soon as we get a couple warm days.

The pond stays crystal clear in the winter and the UGs haven't plugged up in over 3 years. The reason they don't plug is that such a *relatively* small amount of water is being drawn from such a large area (wide matting over the long holey pipes) there isn't enough suction anywhere to plug it up. It works almost by osmosis.

> Osmosis is where a fluid is drawn through an otherwise impermeable membrane on a molecular level. It's the same principle your lungs use to clean the blood of impurities. Talk about serious filtration!

UGs don't really give much mechanical filtration (fish keep the surface of the gravel stirred up) so you still have to use the lava rock filter for that, but there is significant biological activity. The finer the gravel is the greater the surface area for the bacteria to grow on. Probably nowhere near what you get in the lava rock but considerable nonetheless.

> For you techie types - as organic matter is drawn into the gravel and plugs available spaces, it immediately begins to decay. Eventually the space "opens up" again. This is a continually ongoing process and as long as only a relatively small amount of water is drawn through a large area, it will never plug up entirely.

Small Pond UG Filter

If you have a small pond (say a pre-formed one). You can make a pretty nifty little ug filter by taking some 1/2" or 1" plastic pipe, 4 90 degree elbows and a tee. Just make a square or rectangle out of the pipe and elbows (no need to glue anything), drill some holes in the pipes on the inside of the square (It doesn't matter if some of the holes are on the outside though). In one side of the square, insert the tee with a short piece of pipe pointing up. Then wrap the square with several layers of nylon window screening.

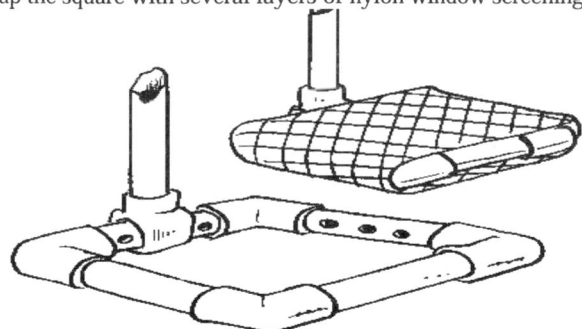

Cover it with gravel. Now all you need is a small air pump and airstone and you have a dandy little filter. Filtration and aeration in one shot. Stick an elbow on top of the stand pipe and you have surface circulation too. This will even work if you cover it with dirt to grow plants in but you're usually better off to grow the plants in pots (see Plants chapter).

Pumps

The most practical pump to use for a first timer is a submersible pump. The advantage to a submersible is they are relatively cheap and easy to install. You can find submersible sump pumps with a decent capacity (say 1,200 gph) for about $60. The disadvantages I've found with sump pumps, though, are they are normally oil sealed and the seals often leak pretty quickly. Even worse they generally don't last too long. They are not designed for 7/24 pumping at full capacity. About a year or less of steady use is usually their upper limit.

The pump I have in my pond now is a large capacity Beckett submersible made specifically for ponds. It's oilless, rated at 3900 gph and costs around $140 at Home Depot. I haven't had it long enough to vouch for its long term durability yet but it's been going more than a year and a half so far. It seems to be much sturdier (heavier, etc.) than the cheaper sump pumps.

Submersible pumps *generally* aren't as efficient the centrifical pumps used typically in swimming pools in terms of gallons pumped, head pressure, etc. for the amount of electricity burned. If you have a large pond, say 4 or 5,000 gallons, and/or are going to pump a great distance (25'+) or height (8'+), it would pay you to look into a swimming pool type pump. But for smaller ponds, the submersible is all you need.

Piping between the pump and the filter can be as simple as a pool hose under the rocks or plants or as elaborate a piping system as you'd like to install. In either case, use as large a diameter (pipe or hose) as is practical. If it's a 1¼" diameter discharge on the pump, use at least 1½ diameter hose or pipe. Up to a point there are major efficiencies to be gained by going up a size that far out weigh the additional cost. This is especially true if there are many bends and turns to make.

If you are in a freeze area and put in "permanent" pipe, make sure it is sloped for good drainage in winter otherwise you'll be repairing/replacing it next spring. Mine is tipped in such a way (over a 20' distance) that all I have to do is disconnect one hose at the filter connection and the whole pipe drains back automatically through the pump into the pond.

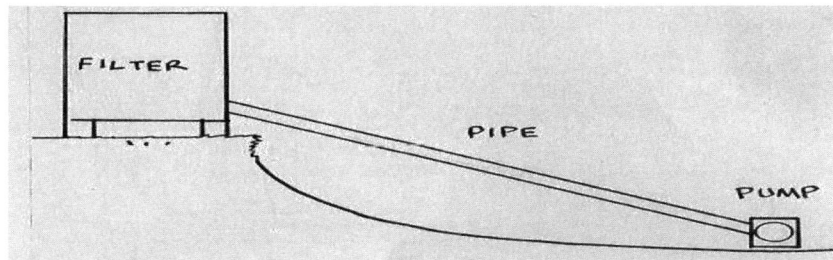

Take the pump out in winter, clean it off well, store it inside and you'll be good to go in the spring. If you don't have an ice forming problem that causes you to lose water in the winter (say on a waterfall), you could just as easily let it run all winter. The only problem is that if you have a pump failure, the pipes could freeze and break.

While we're talking about pipe sizes and efficiency losses this is a good place to mention efficiency loss by virtue of the filter. It's reasonable to believe there will be a large loss due the pumping into the bottom against a 55 gallon drum (or whatever vessel you use for the filter). That's not the case with the lava rock filters discussed here. Look at it as if the barrel were just a section of large hose at the end of the line. There is some loss of efficiency pumping up through the lava rock but it is negligible because the water stream is spread out over such a large area (the entire bottom of the filter container). If the container were the same size as the input pipe, or nearly so, one could have reason to suspect a high loss of efficiency but it's just not the case with the barrel (or 2' x 4' plywood box or ...).

Maximal Circulation.

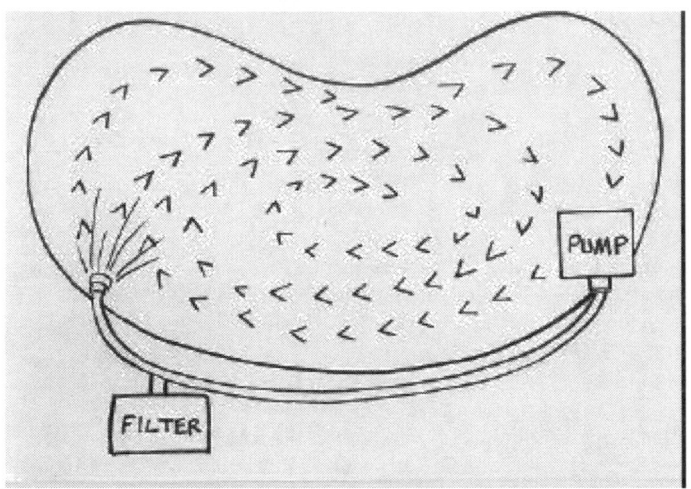

As a general rule you should have the pump located as far away from the
discharge as possible. This to maximize water circulation in the pond. If the
discharge is located near the suction, you are likely to get "dead" areas in the
pond where detritus will accumulate instead of being picked up by the filter.

Electricity

This a good place to talk about electricity. Whatever you do,

DO NOT DO NOT DO NOT USE AN UNPROTECTED OUTLET.

Whatever source you use for power, even if it's only a temporary cord
running from the garage, **MAKE SURE MAKE SURE MAKE SURE** it's

hooked up to a GFI (Ground Fault Interrupted) circuit. This is no place to fool around. Have a qualified electrician run an underground line out to the pond. You should have a 20 amp GFI circuit with several outlets on the end of it. That should be plenty big enough for any more pump(s) (maybe a fountain) and/or lights you'll want later on

> Have the pump hooked up to a switched outlet. It's MUCH more convenient (and professional) than pulling the plug out of an outlet whenever you clean the filter.

Suction Screen

I have my pump inside a plastic bucket. I found an elongated scrub bucket in a K-Mart for $8 that was ideal. The Beckett pump fits in there snugly on its side with the outlet pointing straight up. I then cut a grate out of the trusty old egg crate to fit over the top. (The grate keeps curious fish and leaves out of the suction). Note you don't want to try to "prefilter" too finely here. Using filter padding or something of that nature can be a recipe for disaster. As the padding gets plugged the suction is increased around the edges. (Water has less area to get through.) The suction can get so great as to pull (and kill) fish into it. Best to just use a coarse grate here just to catch the bigger stuff like leaves, etc.

Have a piece of line fastened to the handle of the bucket leading out of the pond or directly to the pump itself if you don't use a bucket. Now whenever you need to clean the pump screen, the whole shebang just lifts right out.

> Never lift the pump by the cord. You may break the seal where the wire goes through the pump housing. You shouldn't pull the pump out by the hose either. It will prematurely weaken the hose.

You will likely eventually find the screen on the pump itself plugging more often than the lava rock filter if you have a large filter relative to the size of the pond. You'll be able to tell by the volume of water coming out of your filter discharge.

An additional advantage to using a bucket is that if you have a pipe or filter failure that causes your pond to be emptied (and it happens, believe me), there should be enough water left in the pond for the fish to survive. You could accomplish the same thing with a float switch that shuts the pump off if the pond gets low but I don't recommend one. It's just one more piece of equipment to maintain and if it fails to work, you will lose all your fish when it pumps the pond dry.

> If you use rigid piping between your pump and the filter, you may need a small section of flexible hose (say 6' of plastic pool hose) between the pump and the piping to allow for easy pump removal and cleaning.

Chapter Three – Waterfalls & Aeration

Waterfalls

Aeration is probably the single most important thing you can add for the health of the pond. Filtering, while important, is more of an esthetic consideration when compared to the efficacy of a waterfall. Waterfalls are valuable addition to a pond. They provide pleasing esthetic values, both visual and audio, and are very healthy for the pond by significantly increasing aeration of pond water. Waterfalls can be in almost any configuration and can be a very good camouflage for the filter.

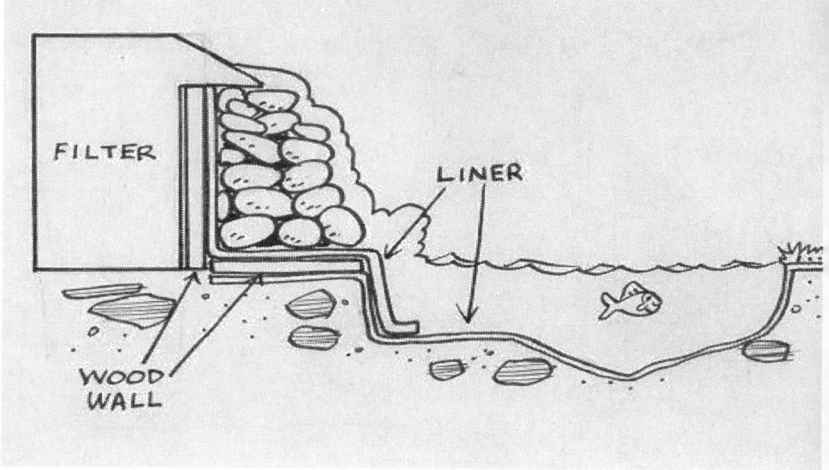

Waterfall as Oxygenator

Oxygen gets used up quickly when breaking down the organic load in the pond (fish wastes, leaves, etc.). Lotsa stuff competing for the available oxygen all at the same time in the water - bacteria, plants, fish, worms, snails, decomposing organics ... The higher the oxygen content that can be maintained, the more bacteria that can be viable and the more efficient the continual cleaning process will be. Waterfalls are a dandy way to keep high oxygen content in the water while giving a great deal of pleasure at the same time.

(Courtesy of Gösta)

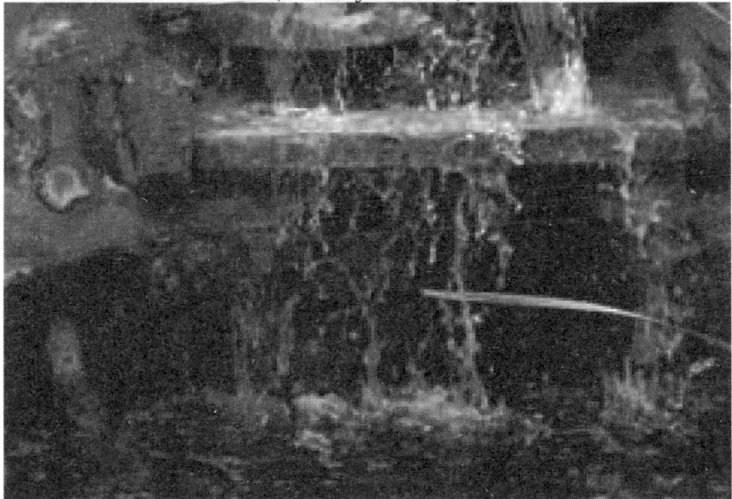

(Unknown)

As you can see there is a lot of continual aeration going on here with both these waterfalls.

You may find the waterfall to be a water hog and lose water due to either splashing outside the confines of the pond or leaking. I have had both those problems. If it happens to you, make sure you stay on the good side of your Kevin (see Miscellaneous chapter) because it's a lot of work taking out those rocks to re-lay the liner underneath or whatever you may have to do.

(Illustration shows a window planter used to distribute the discharge from the filter all across the top of the waterfall rocks.)

The water gets thoroughly aerated and re-oxygenated falling down the wall of rocks. This is healthy for the fish and is another form of filtration (oxidation) as well. The waterfall in my yard gets lots of sun and what happens is that string (filamentous) algae builds up on the rocks and seeds from hanging impatiens drop and bloom in the algae (even more filtration. Looks pretty neat.).

One year I "planted" Parrot Feathers on the top and let them grow down the front. They grow like ... well ... weeds and completely covered the waterfall. That looked pretty neat too. Looked like some sort of 60's ecological afro hairdo.

Using Landscape Rock

For a really rough gauge, you can figure to get 25-30 square feet of vertical coverage from a pallet of flat landscape rocks. Of course you could get a lot more or a lot less too, but it's a ballpark.

Foundation

When you build your waterfall you probably should put it on a foundation of some sort to spread the weight as much as you can. Especially if it is going to be right on the edge of the pond. When the ground gets saturated from a heavy rainfall, it may cause the pond wall to fail, or the waterfall may sag. The foundation doesn't have to be a fancy concrete footing. It can be as simple as a waterfall width of 2"X12" treated lumber dispersing the weight concentrations over a larger area.

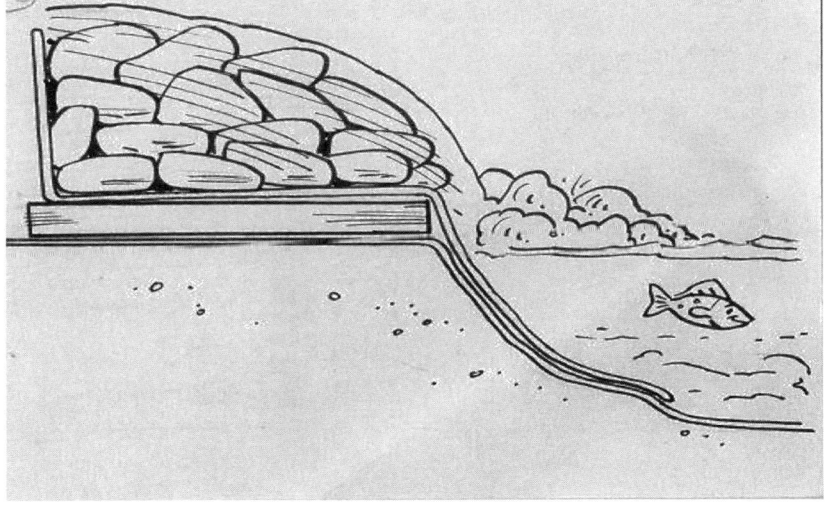

In this illustration you can see how the rocks sit on a 2x12 with a piece of liner behind the rocks and overlapping down into the pond.

Water Losses

Two other factors to keep in mind when building a waterfall are water losses from Splash and Leakage. Splash comes when the water splashes outside the pond. It often doesn't look like much when it's happening but over a period of days it can add up to serious losses. Leakage usually occurs when water makes its way behind the rocks and seeps out instead of being returned to the pond.

Even if you decide to cement your waterfall stones in place, lay a piece of liner underneath and behind. Water has an affinity for finding its way behind the rocks and if it possibly can, it will. I wouldn't want my waterfall cemented just because it's so permanent, if for no other reason. Sometimes you will just want to want to move a rock (or add one or ...) to redirect the water. If they are cemented in that's not possible. Then there's always the (unlikely) chance of some lime or toxic leaching into the water from the cement.

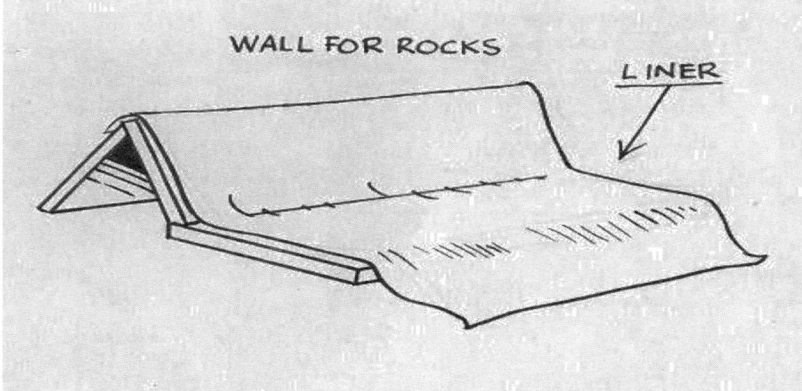

If your waterfall is going to be freestanding, it's best to have it leaning against wall of some kind. You can make a very serviceable wall out of plywood and 2"X4" that will be hidden. *(You may not want as much angle as the exaggerated illustration shows. You will only need to tilt the wall back a few degrees.)*

Waterfall Discharge

Rather than trying to have the water discharge all across the top of your waterfall (as a previous illustration shows), start out by having the discharge all in the center. It will likely spread out to the sides as it makes its way down the face of the waterfall. If you start out all across the top, you will surely find excessive water loss due to splashing. Waterfall direction is an aspect that will likely require considerable tinkering to get "just right".

The location of your waterfall doesn't HAVE to be directly alongside your pond. It can be quite some distance away and connected by a stream you have constructed.

Hiding the Filter behind a Waterfalls

There are probably limitless ways to hide the filter. Below are just pictures of how a couple folks have chosen to hide theirs behind the waterfalls.

(Unknown)
. This one has a stock tank as a filter behind the waterfall.

(Courtesy of Carl)

Behind this waterfall is a 20 gallon barrel. You can just make out the top of the (blue) barrel at the top center of the rocks.

(Courtesy of Trey & Jacques)

And if you have a lot of bricks laying around they can make a stable place to stand while admiring the pond. Notice the cedar covered filter housing in the back feeding the waterfall (below).

Secondary Ponds

If you have plenty room you may want to put in a stream or even a secondary pond. What some folks have done is build a waterfall discharging into a secondary pond which in turn overflows into a stream that meanders back to the main pond. Imagination is your only configuration limit.

Let's talk about a secondary pond first. A lot of people discharge their filter into a small shallow pond, often less than 6" deep, which then overflows into the main pond. This pond is usually made to replicate a small bog and is full of plants (creating a "veggie filter"). The plants act as a natural biological filter, gleaning nutrients from the water before algae can get a foothold.

While shallow ponds make great planting areas, they are not conducive for fish display. Most fish get very nervous in shallow water and as a consequence will be hiding most of the time. You might want to put a few guppies (see Fish chapter) in there in summer to take care of any mosquito larvae though.

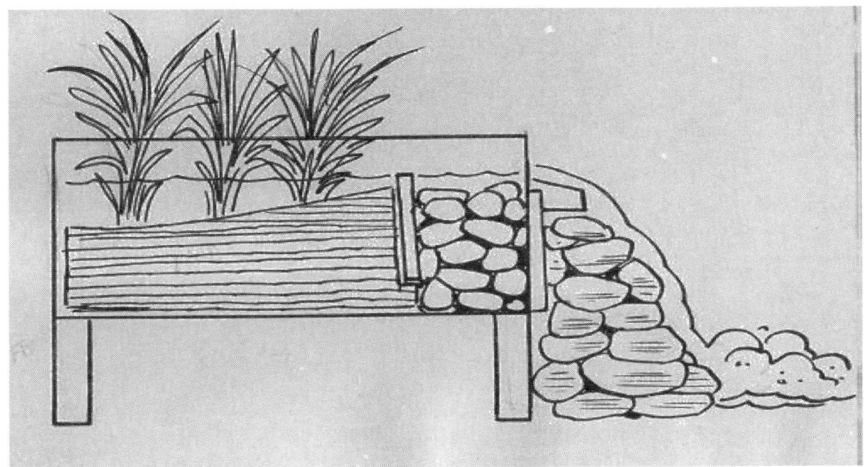

My secondary pond is merely a 6' x 6 x 11" deep tray raised about 40" made out of some old lumber I had around. It sits on legs (actually one end rests on a cleat on a wooden fence) and discharges down the waterfall into the main pond.

The tray is lined with a piece of liner I had left over and has 2" x 2" nailed on top on 3 sides and about half of the fourth. A section about 18" wide is left in the center of the fourth side for the water overflow. In my case I have it discharging down the waterfall . It's about half filled with 6-8" of topsoil mixed with clay sections and covered with 1" of gravel. The topsoil and clay mixture make good planting area for lilies, irises, and the like. The clay makes a sturdy foundation for high growing plants like bog iris to root into. The gravel on top keeps the topsoil and clay from getting stirred up by water movement and washing into the lower pond.

Streams

If you want a stream and have a lot of dirt available from the pond excavation, you can use it to build a raised stream bed and banks for the stream.

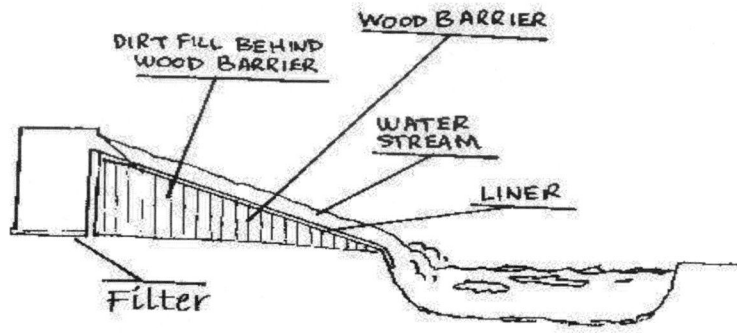

Line the stream bed with liner and cover the liner with stones and gravel to hide it. If there is enough downward angle and flow with the water you can probably get by with overlapping pieces of liner rather than one long piece. *You could probably even get by with one of those waterproof plastic tarps here if the water doesn't pool anywhere, at least to start out with.* A few small "boulders" in the stream would look neat too. Don't make it too wide though. A foot or so should be plenty. A narrow stream will give the illusion of more water moving than a wider one will.

Disrupt the flow of water with stones and rocks as much as you can to get the rippling sound of the water flowing by and to increase aeration. (*You can never have too much aeration {grin}*) The more you can aerate the water the "happier" the pond will be. Two things happen:

1) **To a major extent the oxygen content of the water dictates the health of the water**. The higher the oxygen content, the better it oxidizes organic material in the water ("burns it up").

2) The higher the oxygen content, the healthier the fish will be. In water with a low oxygen content, the fish will be lethargic. Think of it this way. It's the like the difference for us being in a stuffy room and outside in fresh clean air. We have more energy and feel better in clear clean fresh air. If you have a waterfall that splashes into the pond, you will often see fish hanging

around the bottom of it, especially the larger ones. It's not so much they are oxygen deprived as it is they are getting a "boost".

One sure way to tell if you have insufficient oxygen levels is during early morning hours. Many plants are "oxygenators" - they generate oxygen during the day as part of the photosynthesis process but at night they *consume* oxygen, not much but enough to lower the overall content of the pond. If you see your fish, especially the bigger ones, at the surface gasping early in the morning, that's a sure sign of low oxygen levels at night.

Fountains

Fountains are a dandy source of aeration as well, especially if you don't have a waterfall or any kind of splashing arrangement in the discharge from the filter. Home Depot sells a nice array of various small fountain kits in the $40 - $60 range. The only problem I found with them though is they have relatively fine intake strainers and tend to plug quickly, especially if you have a lot of plant life or debris going in the pond. If it has a sponge filter, you can cut a quarter or so off the end so you don't have to clean it as often. (Sponge is also a dandy bacteria base, like lava rock.) Or you may fill the pump cavity with lava rock. When the fountain slows down, just take out the sponge/rocks and clean the pump strainer.

Airstones

If you do suspect that you have insufficient aeration, a cheap way to increase it is to put in an aquarium airstone. Air is a lot lighter than water and it's a whole lot more efficient (cheaper) to pump air than water. A small adequate pump with airstone, hose and all can be gotten for under $15 at a store that sells aquarium supplies. The really small ones won't pump air much over 12" deep though. They just can't put out enough pressure. (Each foot of depth requires nearly ½lb of air pressure to overcome (see *Head*).

Another advantage to an airstone is that it increases water circulation (always a good thing). You even might find your fish frolicking around the bubbles every once in awhile. An airstone is a pretty "maintenance free" item too. Just hook it up and let it go. You may find the stone plugging up after a few months but they're only a couple bucks and easy to change.

Chapter 4 – Fish

Fish costs

As far the price as fish goes - you can spend anywhere from $.10 for a feeder goldfish to five, even six, figures each for fancy imported koi. I'm partial to 10 centers. Put a few dozen feeders in and at least 80% should survive initially. Feeder fish are not bred for their longevity and are often weak when you get them so don't be dismayed if you lose a few. Of the ones that do survive the first few weeks, many will last several years and grow quite big. And with any luck some of them will develop long flowing tails.

Don't put too many or any expensive fish for at least a month or more. Or even the first year. Give your filter time to build up bacteria and let the pond "mature" a little. Another thing to avoid is adding too many fish all at once. It's not likely you will do that at first but don't be tempted to add a lot of large fish at one time. 100 feeders are okay but not more than a few large fish at one time. Each time fish are added, it takes a while (days/weeks) for the bacteria level to adjust to the additional waste load. This is especially true when the bacteriological part of the filter is just getting started. You could easily lose fish by overwhelming the filter before it has time to adjust with a quick buildup of toxic ammonia (a powerful and deadly poison) from the fish waste.

Fish Loading Formula

There are all kinds of formulae to gauge how many fish to put in any given size pond ("1 inch of fish per x gallons of water" or "1 lb of fish per x gallons" or "Calculate the respiration rate of the fish at 72 degrees and measure it against the aeration factor per milliliter per voltmeter" or ...). Stick with feeder fish the first year and only a few of other (cheaper) type fish and you'll soon find what's good for you.

It's been my experience, and I've been through it several times, that it takes a year for a pond to "develop" and start to look like, well, a pond. Another thing from the rueful voice of experience, expect to lose your fish to some sort of catastrophe at least once. It's happened to me two or three times, once with too much chlorinated water at one filling, another when I put unwashed gravel in, another then I took the fish out to expand the pond and the clean {I thought} garbage cans were contaminated; another time ..... So it's best to wait a year or so until things settle in a little, and you get a little experience, before spending too much money on fancy fish. You're surely not as dumb as I am {at least you bought _The Ponder's Bible_ before you started}, but things happen....

If you do lose feeder fish, you can content yourself with the fact they probably had a longer and better quality of life with you than as food for an oscar.

Carp

Almost any member of the carp family will do well. Any of the goldfish, koi, shubunkins, ruyakins, orandas, fantails, and comets will all survive cold winters nicely. Winter mortality is usually well under 10% and is most often 0%. I have them all in my pond and they do well. It isn't a good idea to add fish in cold water (in the winter). It can be quite a shock to them. They will do much better if added in warmer weather months and they get a long gradual adaptation period, say at least a month or two, before really cold weather comes on.

Shubunkins can be very colorful and are a nice addition. If you do add ruyakins don't be alarmed if they just lay on the bottom looking dead for weeks at a time when the water gets cold. They are just "sleeping".

Where to buy fish

If you can, you should buy your fish from a known reputable supplier who maintains his fish in a "medicated quarantined" environment. What that means is he keeps his fish in water that is treated to kill parasites and disease, usually a copper derivative compound of some sort. If you buy fish from a discount outlet or from a place where fish is only a sideline, you run a very real risk of introducing parasites and disease into your pond. *Don't ever buy fish from a cloudy or dirty tank or that has dead fish in it.*

Koi

(A 24" yellow armored or "pine cone" koi in my pond.
The water is 30" deep here so you can see how clear it stays.)

If you're into the wine tasting scene ("Firm but not over powering", "Lascivious but not obscene") look into koi. There are some pretty "exciting"

lineages there and some *very nice looking fish*. Not my cup of tea though.
Koi are very fast growers and will grow quite large, much larger than almost
any other pond fish. I've had them grow as much as 8 or 10" in the first year
and have a couple grow to over 18" in two years. The big fish always brings
the "ohs & ahs".

There are clubs for koi all over the world and many koi shows where
competition is keen. It takes a discerning eye and much experience to judge
koi. I've heard of fish that have sold for well over $100,000 and I'd bet I
couldn't tell the difference between it and a $4 "cull" (what I own). Well I
probably could but you get the idea, it's no place for amateurs on a limited
budget. They're a lot like orchids, you really gotta know what you're looking
at.

One real drawback to koi is they are certain death on (most) plants
and will kill most everything you plant. If you want plants, you'd be well
advised to stay away from koi. *(In the plant section you'll learn a few tricks
to get around their appetite for plants.)*

Tropical Fish

If you live in a temperate area where the water temperature doesn't
go much below 55-60 degrees (he said covetously), you can use pretty much
any kind of tropical fish.

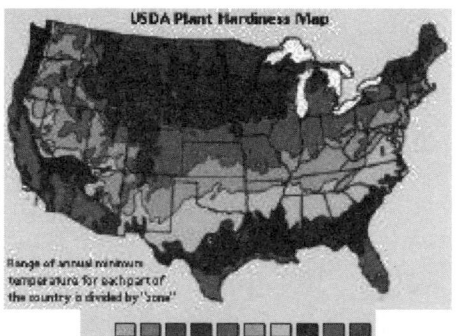

Zone	Centigrade	Fahrenheit	
1	below-46	below -50	
2	-46 to -40	-49 to -40	
3	-41 to -35	-39 to -30	
4	-34 to -28	-29 to -20	
5	-29 to -23	-19 to -10	
6	-23 to -18	-9 to 0	
7	-18 to -13	1 to 10	
8	-12 to -7	11 to 20	
9	-6 to 1		21 to 30
10	2 to 5		31 to 40

(Caution - these are only generalized indicators)

I'd love to have some angelfish in my pond year round but it just gets too cold. I'm at the New Jersey shore where the temperature usually ranges from the teens to the 90's (Fahrenheit) every year (Zone 6) and we've had even more extremes so exotic stuff is out (at least the expensive ones).

You can put tropicals in the pond in the colder zones if the water stays consistently above 60F, as long as you plan to take them out in the early fall before the water starts to cool off too much, say under 65 degrees.

Catching the Fish

The best way I've found to catch them is to not feed them for a few days,
then have the net ready when you first feed them. When they come to the
surface to feed they will be *relatively* easy to catch. That's how I caught
Moby Angel (more on Moby Angel a little later). I had put a $10 bounty on
his head for anyone who could bring him back alive but no collectors. So I
had to resort to trickery, and saved myself $10 in the bargain. He ended up
in my wife's aquarium in school.

Tadpoles

Put some tadpoles in the spring. It's fun to watch them develop into frogs. The frogs will winter okay if they can burrow into the bottom somewhere. Ours don't usually last that long. Iron Ernie eventually gets 'em. Ernie is a cat.

The symbol for iron is FE which stands for Frog Eater. Hence .... Iron Ernie. Oh well, not funny I know but... my cat and my book. I wouldn't recommend bullfrog tadpoles though. They can get quite big and noisy. And will eat the smaller fish. Been there too {sigh}.

Another advantage with 10 centers is that you can over populate, they will find their own balance and you won't be out big bucks. Nothing hurts me more than to lose a $10 or $20 fish.

As soon as the water warms up enough (upper 60's), I usually put a couple bucks worth of feeder guppies in. They thrive and multiply like rabbits all summer and into the fall (except for the year the shiners ate them). Cold water (about 55 degrees) eventually gets the guppies in late fall though.

Golden Orfe (sometimes called Feeder Minnows) are another great and cheap addition to the pond. They add variety and interest and will survive cold winters quite well (but not bullfrogs). If you get orfe try not to get the dark ones. They are not nearly as easy to see as the yellow ones. When your koi get big, they are likely to eat the Golden Orfe.

Catfish

One fish you should avoid is a channel catfish. If you have small fish and put in a small channel catfish, you'll end up with a huge channel cat and a lot fewer small fish. That's what happened to me. I always thought they were vegetarian but I found out that when they reach a certain size, ... well scratch all my minnows, guppies, feeder goldies, etc. before I finally figured the catfish for the culprit one summer. Forget seeing fish getting eaten like you see on those under nature shows. It ain't gonna happen. They're sneaky and fast. Though I did see an angelfish (Moby Angel) mugging up on guppy babies one summer. The baby guppies would hang around the folds of the liner near the surface and Moby Angel was just ambling sideways along picking them off, just like choosing cans of tuna from shelves in a supermarket.

Wild Fish

For a couple years after the Great Chlorination Kill, I had a small mouth bass and 2 or 3 sunnies in the pond my Kevin had caught in a local lake. While they were neat when you saw them (which wasn't often), they weren't much fun. It was kind of fun catching grasshoppers and other bugs to feed them but that was about it. The bass especially was neat. Drop a grasshopper in the pond and bass would appear out of nowhere, have the hopper, and disappear in under a split second.

Chapter Four – Fish

Wild fish tend to be very quiet. It's how they conserve energy in the low food conditions usually found in the wild. An even bigger drawback for me was the normally low visibility of the wild fish. They are natural "hiders". They are always under rocks or behind plants or hiding somewhere. It's a natural instinct in the wild to keep from becoming food for somebody else.

I had a few bigger goldfish in with them too and they always seemed "nervous". They were quiet and just didn't seem to swim around like they normally did before the wild bunch showed up. Something else too, any small fish (10 centers, golden orfes, etc) had a very short life span. I don't know if it was the sunnies or the bass but they didn't last long.

Some people keep wild fish in their ponds like rainbow trout, whitefish suckers, pickeral and the like, but most don't have too much luck. The water can get quite warm in the summer, especially if the pond gets a lot of sun, and many wild fish cannot tolerate the heat. They are used to being in cool stream water in the mountains. I've got a few suckers in my pond and when the water gets much above 80 degrees, I always lose one or two. I really don't know how many are in there because they are hiders and the only time I've ever seen them (since putting them in) is when they die of "heat stroke". Trout, for example, are said to expire at water temps above 70F.

Once I put in a quart of killies and a few dozen shiners (bait fish from the local tackle shop). I don't think I'll put them in again though, they're aggressive eaters and the rest of the fish consequently get fewer opportunities. Besides I saw them eating my guppies, a real NO NO. They don't seem to have the longevity of the goldfish (most died within a year) and aren't nearly as attractive.

I had the sunnies and the bass a year or so and it ended up costing me $20 to get a neighbor kid to catch them and return them to the lake so I could get back to my 10 centers.

Fish Food

Primarily I feed my fish dried cat food. It's cheap and nutritious. Every once in a while, I'll throw in a Milk Bone. It's fun watching them nibble away at it. I give them normal fish food too but that's like a treat. (I prefer the TETRA brand flakes, have had very good luck with it in my aquariums). I always have Friskies cat food on hand, and usually buy Whiskas for the fish. Whiskas is a lot smaller pieces and is easier to eat for the smaller fish.

I feed my boys a lot. Any time I don't see any more food floating, I throw in another handful of Whiskas or Friskies. Winter time too though they don't seem to eat near as much. I've heard a lot of claims about only feeding once or twice a day and then only as much as they'll eat in 2 or 5 minutes but I don't subscribe to it (though I do in my Salt water tank). Under that theory, the big dogs get to eat the most and the little guys hardly get anything. My way they all get as much as they want. (That's yet another good reason to have an oversize filter system. No worries about overfeeding generating excess fish waste or rotting food souring the water.)

Besides the Friskies, I have a small plastic bucket (about 2 qts) filled with a mixture of: a cup of Tetramin Pond sticks, a cup of Tetramin Fish Flakes, a handful of Friskies, and a couple handfuls of some puppy dog food that looks like gray Cheerios. I mix it up a little and the flakes get ground into a fine powder. The Friskies and pond sticks float, the "cheerios" sink and the flakes do both. That way all sizes get something and a good rich varied diet. They get a handful of this once or twice a day or more or whenever I just want to see them swarming.

Often I'll feed them Whiskas 5 or 6 times in a day, or even more in the summer. (It isn't necessary to be so anal, I'm retired and just don't have a whole lot else to do. Besides it's easy to grab a handful of out of the cats' bucket and toss it off the porch into the pond.)

Fish Food Costs

I did a cost comparison of various fish foods and compared protein content. Dried cat food, by far, came out the most cost effective for just protein content. A $40 bucket of pond sticks would hardly last the summer. $10 worth of cat food lasts near the whole year (We buy Friskies by the 20lb bag for the cats for about 50 cents a pound. Whiskas is even cheaper, $7 for 17 lbs.). Start figuring out the protein cost of other food sources and it can run over $75 a lb in a small can of flakes (7 oz of 40% protein for $15) compared to less than $1.50 lb in 30% protein in cat food. Other things to consider sure but ...

Growth Rates
Another neat thing to watch with 10 centers is the varying growth rates. They will be all the same size when you buy them and in a few weeks you would swear they couldn't all be from the same brood. Then if you watch, pretty soon one will get big enough to where he can swallow a whole Frisky instead on just nibbling at it. When that happens you can almost see him grow for awhile and he will get monstrous compared to the others. The rest will catch up over the next year or so.

Get them to eat out of your hand.
Koi especially can be trained to eat out of your hand if you have the patience. Feed them the same place every day at the same time(s) by holding the food in your hand, then putting it into the water and letting go. Pretty soon they will get accustomed to the routine and be anticipating you, Next thing they will be eating out of your hand. Even nibble "the hand that feeds them" {grin}.

Fish & Birds

If you find your fish have all of a sudden gotten very nervous and hide a lot, you likely have an early morning breakfast visitor. It may very well be a heron or stork. If it is, you can provide some protection for your fish by tossing in some 2' sections of 4-6" plastic drainage pipe for them to hide in. It's pretty cheap ($2 for 8' at a home center). Better yet is to take some plastic coated wire mesh and fashion it into a "tunnel". The advantage to a mesh tunnel is the fish are protected but you can still see them.

Fish in Winter

You don't have to, and probably shouldn't, bring your fish in for the winter. All members of Carp family will do just fine outdoors. As the temperature falls their metabolism slows right down until they go almost dormant. When the water gets near freezing, they stay almost motionless in the water. I feed my fish in the winter but not very much. I'll throw a handful of Friskies on the water and it may take several days for it to all disappear in the cold of January and February.

> As a matter of interest, it seems carp (and a few other species) have an ability to generate a sort of antifreeze in cold water. It has recently become a subject of scientific inquiry. Dunno why, I certainly am not interested in getting cold enough where I would want my body to have to generate antifreeze.

Many authorities advocate stopping feeding as soon as the water goes below 50 degrees. Their reasoning is the metabolism of the fish is too slow to digest the food and it will sour in their stomachs. I don't hold with that. These species of fish have been around for 1,000's of years before humans domesticated them (only a hundred years or so). If eating in cold weather was damaging to them they would long ago stopped eating on their own. One guy had me so convinced of this one year I went out and bought about 20 boxes of Epsom Salts (an old fashioned "physic") and put in the pond. Trying to "clean them out" before it was too late, you see. Didn't seem to hurt the fish any but I had a pretty good slug of "skinny worms" laying on the bottom for awhile (and snickers from a few of the local ponders).

In either case, it doesn't hurt to feed them or not feed them when the water is cold (say under 50F or 10c). Generally fish are extraordinarily efficient eaters and can go long periods - weeks, even months if the water is cold enough. The reason they can do that is the species originated in a hostile environment where available food was only sporadic at best so they had to develop a survival mechanism to deal with it. The way they do it is to rapidly digest food when it is available and efficiently store it (in the form of fat) so that it's available for energy when ready food is scarce. Further it takes very little energy for fish to survive. They are essentially weightless so stored fat goes a long way.

Parasites

Parasites inevitably come to everybody's pond/aquarium sooner or later. The most common by far of these is called ICH. It is usually manifested as small white spots on the skin and fins of the fish. ICH is often fatal to smaller fish like small goldfish and even occasionally to larger fish like koi. What happens is that damage to the skin gets an infection and/or damage to the gills renders them ineffective. In either case, death can result.

ICH is often present in the pond (some authorities say always) and the resident fish have developed a resistance to it but can have an outbreak when there is a sudden environmental insult or shift (say a sudden water temperature change) or the fish get stressed for some reason. ICH can live under the skin/scales of a resistant fish for long periods. ICH is infectious and can spread to other fish (even previously resistant fish) if a newly acquired non-resistant fish is added to the pond and it contracts it.

The first line of defense against an outbreak of ICH is a salt treatment (*see Water Quality in Chapter 5 for dosages*). If it doesn't clear up in a couple weeks you will have to go to stronger medication. Water temperature plays a big role in the longevity of ICH. It can live months in colder water. See your local pond or aquarium store for their recommendation. There's just too much medication out there today for me to mention any here.

Another ICH treatment is to raise the water temperature. Supposedly ICH will not survive above 80 or 85F degrees (27 to 29C) but artificially warming the water is usually not practical in a pond. One possibility is to remove the infected fish as soon as you can and isolate him/them in a small separate aquarium where you can treat them more effectively.

ICH propagate by dropping small "eggs" (they're not technically eggs but close enough for our purposes here) that sink to the pond bottom. Prevention can be practiced by having good circulation and filtration in the pond, especially on the bottom. Larger active fish create bottom circulation just by scavenging the bottom, stirring up ICH "eggs" the filter will catch.

Fish Ulcerations

Ulcerations on the body of fish can be caused by several things: First and foremost are infections. Again salt is the first line of defense here. If the ulcerations continue after a salt treatment or two, then you will have to go a medication. The ulcer may not be bacterial or parasitic based though but a fungus instead. There is no easy way for a layman to determine what kind of ulcer it is. Again there are a lot medications available today but the one time I had a persistent problem with ulcers on a lot of my fish , my aquarium guy recommended a product from Jungle Labs called "Fungus Eliminator" ($12 for 500 gals treatment). It did the trick for me and cleared the ulcers right up in a week or two in almost all the fish. I was some glad too. I was thinking it was a parasite but I guess not. Was figuring I was gonna have to let the fish all die and drain the pond to kill it (the parasitic infection).

Chapter 5 – Water Quality

Water quality could be a whole book or two in itself but don't worry, we won't too technical here. I'll start right from the beginning, the first fill of the pond.

The first fill

When you first fill the pond it's a good idea to let it sit awhile (hours or overnight), keep the pump running to get a good thorough circulation and then pump it out.

This is especially true if you have gravel and/or rocks in the pond. Any contaminates in the material have a chance to wash off and/or dissolve in the water. If you have gravel on the bottom (and I hope you do), take a push broom or a rake with the tines pointing upward (so as not to puncture the liner) and work the gravel while pumping out.

This should get rid of the gravel dust. If the dust is severe, you may have to flush it several times. Note you don't have to fill it to the top of the pond to flush the gravel, a couple inches of water over the gravel should be enough. You don't have to go nuts if it's still a little "dusty" after flushing it several

times. Let it sit overnight with the pump running for circulation and if the
dust has settled out by the morning it should be okay.

Most likely you will be using chlorinated city water, so it's recommended
you always use a spray nozzle when filling. Even if you are using well water
it's likely to be low in oxygen. (discussed next.)

It's not really necessary but it will accelerate the dissipation of the chlorine
and more quickly oxygenate the water. Chlorine will normally dissipate over
a 24 hour period by itself but it doesn't hurt to help it along. In some (few)
areas other chemicals beside chlorine (maybe chloramine compounds) are
used to purify city water and they may not dissipate naturally, or as readily
or easily. If you suspect that's the case in your area, call the water company
to find out what you have to do to disperse them. If it's a big involved
process involving expensive filters, etc. I'd wait for awhile before getting
involved with it. You just might be able to get by without the expense. (If
your 10 centers do okay over time, say a few months, then it's very likely
everything else will too.)

If you are using a shallow ground well (and I am), there might be a sour odor
to the water. This comes from organics in the water that haven't been
oxidized. What happens is that organics get washed into the ground during a
rain and quickly use up the available oxygen in the groundwater. There is

little or no exposure to the air to replenish the oxygen used up so the water smells. As soon as the oxygen gets replenished by circulating in the pond the odor should soon go away, usually in a couple hours.

Circulation

In either case (city or well water) you should let your pump run getting as much circulation as you can for 12-24 hours after the first fill before adding any fish or plants. Put the pump at one end and the discharge hose at the other.

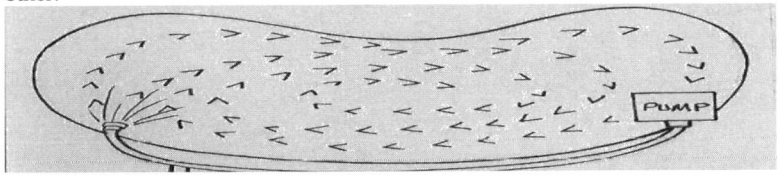

Later on, after you get the pond established, be a little careful if you are replacing evaporation or replacing a large percentage of the pond. I once turned the hose on (was using city water then) and forgot it overnight. The next morning nearly a hundred (four year old) gold fish were dead floating on top of the water. Now that will make you sick, believe me. So don't put too much chlorinated water in at one time if you have fish (it probably won't do your plants any good either), certainly no more than 50% of the pond volume, and try to use a spray nozzle (I wasn't). A trick I use now is to set the kitchen timer for a reminder so I don't forget the hose is on.

Evaporation

You will have to replace the water that evaporates, probably at least weekly. Some days it seems like the pond will go down a couple inches and other times it will go weeks before you have to add water. It all depends on the weather (what doesn't?). Only H2O (pure water) evaporates and leaves behind any compounds or chemicals that may have been in it when it was added to the pond, plus any that are added from fish food, plant food, rain, etc.

Actually you will likely lose less than ¼" a day to evaporation, certainly less than ½. Losing more than that to evaporation is very unlikely even in the driest weather or climate. If the pond level drops noticeably you can be pretty sure you are losing water somewhere else.

The compounds left behind accumulate, and if not attended to, will eventually very likely concentrate and make the pond toxic. Many ponders recommend removing and replacing 10% of the water every week because of the residual effects of evaporation. (The 10% "rule" has its roots in aquarium keeping.) That would be in addition to water lost to evaporation. What that does is keep any possibly accumulating toxics from rising to poisonous levels. I let the pond overflow when I am (re)filling it. Is it exactly 10%? I don't know but seems enough. Heavy rains that cause the pond to overflow have the same effect of diluting the possible toxins.

Oxygen Capacity of water

An important fact to remember throughout your pondering career is that as water warms it rapidly loses its capacity to hold oxygen. I don't remember the actual numbers but it is very dramatic, almost logarithmic, something like water holding 2 or 3 times more oxygen at 50 degrees than it does at 60 degrees. And the warmer the water gets, the less oxygen it holds, so aeration is important (even critical), not only if you like high populations of fish, but for the biological aspects of the filter systems of the pond (both natural and manmade).

Oxygen saturation occurs somewhere around 9 ppm (depending on temperature) with the norm being around 6 ppm. Fish start to get nervous near 5 ppm, will get stressed under that and will likely die when oxygen gets under 2 ppm. The larger fish are affected first. When you consider that we normally have something like 230,000 ppm of oxygen in our air to live on, you can appreciate the dramatic need for aeration in the pond. Even if we only have a few fish in a relatively large area, it will almost certainly be a far higher concentration on a fish per gallon ratio than occurs in nature.

pH

pH is the abbreviation for *potentia hydrogenii*, a concentration of hydrogen ions in water. It's measured on a scale of 0-14 but the range we are concerned with runs from about 6.5 to 8 with 7 being considered neutral. The pH scale is logarithmic which means each full point represents a 10-fold change in pH measurement. Below 7 means the water is *acidic* and above 7 means it is *basic* or alkaline.

As a rule of thumb, carp will do well in water that is a little alkaline (say between 7 and under 8). They can do okay a little on either side of that range (maybe even as much as a point) but they thrive best at a little above 7. Plants do okay there too but some of them are very sensitive to pH and require a fairly specific range to prosper. Just like orchids need a different soil and fertilizer than tomatoes for example.

Reasonably reliable pH testing kits are about $10 at aquarium stores. If your test kit gives wild readings (very low or very high), test it on different sources of water (tap water vs pond water for example) which should not yield exactly the same readings. It may be the kit was improperly stored or shipped (maybe frozen) and is unreliable.

Don't go nuts over small changes in pH though unless you are into show fish or show plants. It's not at all unusual for pH to vary from morning to night (say several tenths, even as much a full point, though that would be unusual), due to the respiration of plants and fish, varying oxygen levels, etc. Any number of factors (rain, leaves, runoff, water...) affect pH as well.

If the source water is within a reasonable range and you do periodic water changes (discussed above) you shouldn't have a problem with pH. It's sort of like your blood pressure. It can vary considerably within a reasonable range but as long as it's not consistently high or low it's generally okay.

Good aeration (have I mentioned aeration yet?) goes a long way to moderating (or *buffering*) pH. Most folks won't have pH problems but if your pond tests consistently low (acidic) say under 6.5, you could try to raise it with baking soda, limestone or some other mechanism. Or if it is over 8.5 (alkaline) then you could probably try to lower it with muriatic acid or oak leaves or ... Try to spread the alteration over days/weeks in order to avoid stressing the fish with a rapid change. In other words don't try to change it overnight. In either case if you have ready access to crushed clam/oyster shells, it wouldn't hurt to place a bunch in your filter stream or pond bottom. It will have a stabilizing effect (buffering pH swings) by bringing down abnormally high pH and raising low pH.

The odds are most likely you won't have a pH problem. Most folks don't unless they get into show quality fish and plants.

Thermoclines

You've probably heard the term "thermocline" (distinct layers of water of sharply different temperatures). In a shallow pond I don't believe there's such a thing. The subsurface temperature will vary only slightly from the temperature on the bottom. I leave my UG filters going all winter which mixes top and bottom water continually and have seen no adverse effects on my fish.

A thermocline might be a factor in a deep pond or lake but has no effect on a shallow pond like we're building here. Nor should it affect the fish in any negative way.

Limiting Factor

Limiting Factor is a biological term which simply means (in our case) a nutrient which, when used up, limits the growth or expansion of an organism. A simple example would be a particular plant requiring potash, phosphorus and nitrogen to grow (three main nutrients for most plants). If its environment contains all three, the plant will proliferate until there is no more room or it runs out one of the three elements. If the potash is used up, it can't grow anymore until it finds new potash. In this case potash is said to be the *limiting factor*. If it runs out of room to expand before depleting the three nutrients then room is said to be the *limiting factor*.

Fish generate nitrogen derivatives and phosphorus, (as well as ammonia) in their waste and respiration so there is usually plenty of both in the water. Algae (especially the water discoloring kind) require phosphorus to grow and proliferate, so phosphorus *can* be a limiting factor for algae. The trick is to get something that will use the phosphorus first before the water algae get a chance to use it to get established. Water hyacinths, as prolific growers, are very good at quickly sucking up phosphorus and other nutrients. (More on plants later.)

They (and not just hyacinth) serve to limit or inhibit algae growth two ways:

1) The algae need sunlight, phosphorus, etc. to get established and the hyacinth is *already established* so it gets to the phosphorus first. They use up necessary (to the algae) phosphorus before the algae have a chance at it.

2) The leaves of the hyacinth block the sun from the algae the algae needs to grow or even get established. By reducing the amount of sun available to the pond water there can be less algae production even if there were enough other nutrients. *The sun (or more specifically lack of) becomes the limiting factor.*

Many pond professionals recommend at least half to two thirds of the pond be shaded with water plants so that the combination of low sunlight availability and the nutrient uptake of the plants keep algae growth in check. This formula can work quite well in a "natural" pond with little or no external filtration and a low fish load. There is no need of having that much shade in a well filtered pond though (unless you want it).

Freezing

Ice in winter is a problem for many ponders. Pond professionals generally recommend keeping at least a small hole in the pond ice free, otherwise toxic gases can build up from fish respiration and decaying organics. There are any number of ways to do that with small pond heaters being the best way. A small heater (under 100 watts), with a built-in thermostat so it doesn't turn on until the water is cold enough to freeze, sits on or near the surface. Some very efficient pond heaters sell for under $50 so if you think you need one, it pays to shop around (what doesn't?).

Another solution is to leave something floating in the middle of the pond. A small log perhaps, or as has been suggested by one net surfer, use the lid from an ice chest with a hole poked in the middle. Tie a container of stones to it to keep it from blowing around.

What I do is leave my UG filters going all winter so there is always a little surface circulation which usually keeps a fair sized section of the pond open. The pond surface will freeze over completely if there is an extended freeze, say several days well below freezing in a row, but it clears quickly as soon as we get a couple warmer days.

Another method to use is to use an air bubbler, which keeps the surface disturbed but that will freeze over eventually too. What happens is that as the bubbles burst the mist freezes and builds up around the hole until it eventually coves the hole like a small overturned bowl.

For years I had nothing (heater or pump running) and the pond would stay frozen over for a month or more at a time in January and February. I had no fish mortality to speak of then. The gas buildup may be more of a factor in ponds with a high organic load (leaves, etc.) decomposing or where ice cover is several months long. It's not something I ever had a problem with.

Salt

Salt is a cheap efficient additive for ponds. The blood of fresh water fish is between .5% and 1% salt and of course fresh water contains little or no salt. As a result fish lose salt naturally as a result of respiration and salt can become deficient in their systems and they will get stressed if they can't replace it from the water itself (called "osmo-regulating") or through the food they eat. Also many fresh water parasites, funguses and diseases cannot live in salted water and will die if salt is added to the pond.

Just how much salt, and the right kind, to add is a problem. Salt is harmful to some plants in low dosages and obviously will kill the fish and plants in high dosages. First of all, don't use ordinary table salt. It's *iodized* and will harm your pond life. Use non-iodized, naturally occurring salt. Sea salt used in salt water aquariums is an excellent source (it contains many essential micro-elements). But it is very very expensive, as much as $1.50 a lb. Road salt, such as is sold in winter to melt driveway ice, is a good source and is quite cheap, often under 10 cents a lb. Read the label carefully to make sure it is "natural" and has no additives though (some does). Another source for salt is from a plumbing store (unlikely as it sounds). They sell salt for water purifiers and it's usually pretty reasonable.

A rule of thumb for adding salt is 1 lb for each 100 gallons of water as a "normal" treatment and as much as 3 lbs per 100 gallons if you have a parasite infestation (such as ICH). At the upper levels, you may kill the water lilies and other plants so be a little careful when adding it. If you think you need the higher levels (due to infestation or lesions on the fish), add it gradually over several days to avoid sudden shock. Remove any water lilies or other plants until the problem clears and you can do a (series of) water change(s). (Remember the salt will stay in the water like any other element and become concentrated through evaporation.)

A low concentration of salt (say up to 1 lb per 100 gallons) is healthy for the pond and fish and can go a long way in keeping your pond healthy and is recommended as a maintenance dose.

Chapter 6 – Flowers & Fauna

Just as there is a huge selection of plants for your garden, there is a pretty fair selection of plants for ponds with more becoming available every year as the ponding hobby grows. You may want to consider having one end or section of the pond 8" or a foot or so deeper than the rest –

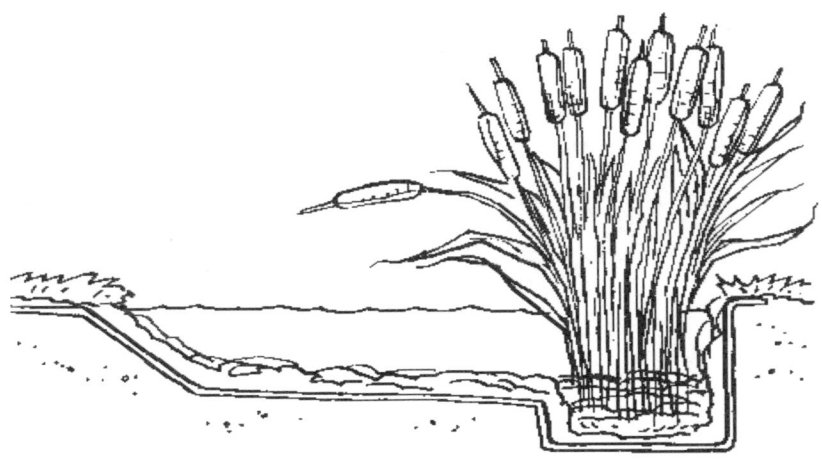

and have it filled in with topsoil and/or clay. It provides a place for plants to root naturally, especially if they propagate say like sagitteria. Others may be better in pots for the pond so as to limit their spread otherwise they tend to take over. Cattails (even though depicted in the illustration as uncontained) have an amazingly aggressive root structure.

Many plants grow well in pots or even free floating. A big advantage to pots is that you can easily move the plants as your mood dictates. The hardy varieties, for example, can be moved into deeper water to winter over, then back in the spring or summer to take advantage of the sunlight to flower. The tropical varieties can be moved inside for the winter.

Water lilies

A hardy lily

Water lilies are the plant most identified with ponds. Lilies come in all shapes and sizes with pads (leaves) the size of a silver dollar to as high as three feet across in some show varieties. Water lilies come in two broad classifications - hardy and tropical. Hardy means it will winter well in cold water. Tropical means it will die in extended cold water (under 50 degrees) and so has to be brought in by the first frost. Generally the tropicals are the most colorful, offer the most varieties and yield the most flowers. But they are the most expensive and the most difficult (read work) to winter over.

A hardy lily

The best bet with lilies is to plant them in wide individual, relatively shallow pots in a clay or sandy type soil. Lilies generally aren't fussy and they will do well in mud or gravel as well. You can use topsoil to plant them in but don't use potting dirt. Potting soil usually has a lot of synthetic pellets in it to keep the soil aerated that will float out. Lilies will even grow in a very coarse mesh bag with a rock in it to hold it on the bottom. (The pads and flowers just poke their way through the meshes on the way to the surface and the bags keep away destructive koi.)

Many lilies will do as well in a few inches of water as they do in 30" but it's generally best to keep them in about the 6-18" depth range. If you haven't made shelves for the plants to sit on when you dug the pond and the water is relatively deep, you can set the pots on milk crates. Or make little tables of ½ PVC pipe for legs and some egg crate for the "table top" to hold them nearer the surface. If they are too close to the surface the pads don't spread well.

To winterize hardy lilies, all you have to do is move them to the bottom of deepest part of the pond and they will winter fine. Tropicals require being brought in, trimmed back, usually covered, and kept in a warmish place. And even that is not always successful. If you buy tropicals, be sure to get explicit instructions for them from the supplier.

When you buy the lilies (from as little as $6-$8 to quite expensive - $25 and up) you will almost assuredly get planting and care instructions with them. Don't go overboard the first year though, one or two is plenty until you see how they prosper. Many types have large pads, often as big as a small dinner plate, and can put out as many as two dozen pads at a time. Pads are constantly coming up to replace the existing ones as they die off. If you can reach a pad easily when you see it starting to die (turning brown), nip it and take it out. Plenty more where it came from.

Most lilies only put out one flower at a time and it normally only lasts a few days. Again there are many varieties of water lily and they all have different characteristics (some flower more prolifically than others or differently, only at a certain time of day or season for example). They are not great water filters though, not nearly as good as some other plants we'll be discussing later. There is, though, a fine "hair" on the bottom of the pads that gathers fine particulate and you will occasionally see fish plucking tasty snacks from it.

The lily leaves provide a great deal of shade per plant and you will often find the fish resting under them on a hot sunny day. Speaking of the sun, lilies love lots of it, the more the better. Most won't flower in the shade. Another advantage of the large leaves is they tend to protect the pond from rapid temperature changes between a hot day and a cool night. Frogs like to sit on the pads and wait for insects during the day.

It's usually recommended to put a fertilizer tab or two in each lily pot once a month in the summer flowering period. While I don't think it's absolutely necessary (we'll talk about pond fertilizing a little later on in this chapter), like Grandma's chicken soup, what could it hurt? Speaking of fertilizer tabs, no need to buy expensive pond specific tabs. Plant fertilizer spikes are generally cheaper and will work fine.

Water Hyacinth

Water hyacinth

Water hyacinth are prolific growers and will propagate wildly if uncontrolled. For that purpose they are outlawed in many places as a noxious weed in the warmer climates. They have been known to completely overwhelm large lakes, even slow moving rivers. A couple places in Africa and South America even harvest it for animal fodder.

Water hyacinth has a dense root structure that hangs just below the floating plant. This root structure is what voraciously soaks up nutrients in the water and gives it its fast growth. It makes a great, if incomplete, biological filter. The roots also pick up and hold particulates and provide a haven for small fish (guppies, etc). If the fish spawn the eggs sometimes attach themselves to the roots as well. It *sometimes* puts out a gorgeous flower, but it only lasts for one day.

It makes a nice addition to the pond but you have to keep pruning it back or you will wake up one day to find it taking over. Hyacinth are usually pretty cheap ($2-$5 range) and you only need one or two to get started. A few weeks of warm sunny weather and it'll start to take off if there are enough nutrients. You'll soon be able to go into the water hyacinth selling business. Keep in mind though, water hyacinth will die as soon as the water gets cold. Lots of good things about hyacinth.

Parrot Feathers

Parrot feathers are a cute little floater plant that is another prolific grower. It can grow a pretty fair size root structure (not near as much as the hyacinth though). It sticks up out of the water a couple inches and looks like neat little pine trees. The roots will reach down in shallow water to take hold wherever they can. A friend had his pump laying only about 12" below the surface and the parrot feathers had reached down and infiltrated the intake screen and impeller section so tightly he needed a screwdriver to pry them all out.

I usually put some parrot feathers on the top of my waterfall in the spring. One year we went away for a couple weeks in early July and when we came back it had covered the entire waterfall and the top pond. Looked like some sort of Amazon jungle or a huge green 60's afro. Parrot feathers will stand some mildly cold weather but die out in the winter. You can keep them inside as long as they get at least an hour of sun every day. They are pretty cheap (as little as $2 mail order) and that's about all it takes to get started.

Anacharis

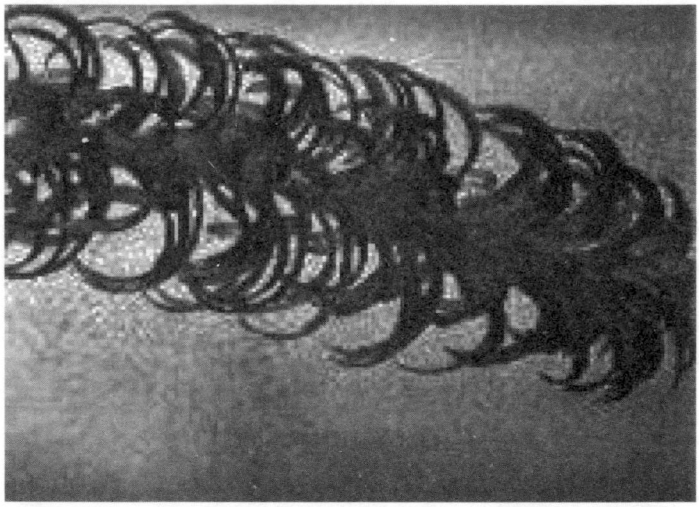

Anacharis is a floating plant that does well in ponds. It doesn't have much of a root structure when floating but will put out some fine roots when planted. When it's happy, it will reward you with tiny delicate white flowers. A good grower but not intrusive like hyacinth or parrot feathers. If it doesn't get eaten by the fish, it will take several years to become a nuisance, if at all. Anacharis sinks to bottom in cold water and will winter okay. When the water warms it makes its way back to the top. It is a good little oxygenator too (it adds more oxygen to the water than it uses). It looks something like a dark green test tube brush. Anacharis usually sells for about $2 a bunch in aquarium shops and mail order. ("Bunch" sizes may vary though.) It is less than 1 inch across and can grow as long as a foot or more.

Hornwart

Hornwart is another good, but not intrusive grower. It is a mid water floater and looks like light green tumbleweed. It too will winter okay and return in the spring or early summer. A big advantage to hornwart is that it makes a dandy haven for small fish and juveniles. Hornwart is priced and sold similarly to Anacharis.

Sagittaria

There are numerous subspecies of sagittaria and many/most will take root and spread in mud bottoms. Some varieties will grow has much as 3-4' high sticking up out the water and putting out delicate tiny white flowers. As it spawns it will cover the water with a yellow "dust" that sinks to the bottom to take root. It will have to be trimmed back every year or so but provides fine cover for the fish. Sagittaria is a very nice addition to "koi-less" ponds. Sagittaria is priced and sold similarly to Anacharis.

Cattails

Wild cattails do well in a pond but they should be contained in a large pot. If they aren't they will take root in the gravel or mud bottom and develop an astonishingly extensive root structure and spread out fairly rapidly over the next year or two, putting up new plants as they go. They can grow quite tall (6' or more) if they can develop the root structure to support themselves. I suppose you can buy them but they are very cheap if there is a marshland nearby and you can pick your own.

(Courtesy of Carl)

As you can make out from the picture these cattails are jammed into the pot as tight as they can get. It started out as one but quickly expanded to fill the pot.

Duckweed

Duckweed is a tiny little floater about ¼" across. A prolific grower in quiet water, it can get intrusive if there are no fish to eat it. It grows quite well in my top pond and when it gets to be too much up there, I scoop some out and toss it into the main pond. The fish love it and it disappears quickly. There is a school of thought that holds you shouldn't feed the fish plants that have grown in the pond. The reasoning is the plants have an uptake of various nutrients and by feeding the plants to the fish, the nutrients are returned to the pond thereby negating the filtering good the plants have done. That may very well be true but it goes a bit far for me.

Very often plants you buy (if you get them from an outdoor source) will have duckweed sticking to them, which is enough for it to get a foothold if there are no fish around to eat it. I suppose you can buy it but ...

Other plants

There are almost as many varieties of plants for the pond as there is for the garden. Seems like it anyway, The best bet is to get catalogs from some of the sources listed in the References Chapter. Shop around a little as prices can vary a great deal, especially for the higher priced stuff. Often the same plants sold for aquariums will do well in the pond in warm water months. You just have to try them out and see.

Don't be afraid to try (a few) house plants or ornamentals sitting in shallow water (a couple inches deep) for the summer. Some will do very well. I have even have tossed the "babies" from a Spider plant in the pond itself and they have survived okay. The koi don't even seem to bother them.

Algae

The last plant I'll talk about is Algae. Mostly I've covered the water borne algae (microscopic phytoplankton) that discolors the water. But there are many other kinds that will show up in the pond.

If you have a waterfall or a pond with few or no fish in it, you may get an (unsightly?) explosion of algae that looks like fine angel hair that is put on Christmas trees. It's called, appropriately enough, Hair Algae. It grows in long stringy tenacles down the front of the waterfall and looks and feels like cotton candy underwater. It can get quite thick, even so thick as to "suffocate" other plants like liles, etc.. What I do when it gets thick in my shallow secondary pond is scoop it up and toss the clumps right into the main pond. (A litter box scoop that looks like a miniature pitchfork works really well.) The fish soon make short order of it. I figure it's just like feeding spinach to the kids. Fresh vegetables and all that.

If you have a lot of anacharis or water cress they will tend to hold down on string (or hair) algae as they will utilize the growing nutrients first (to some extent).

Another type of algae you'll see is a dark greenish slime that grows on all the underwater surfaces of the pond.

Do be concerned with these last two types unless they obviously get out of hand. Growing algae acts like a veggie filter soaking up nutrients just like any other plants. It's a sign of a healthy pond.

Snails

As often as not some plants you buy will have a snail or two attached somewhere. This is not a cause to worry. Snails are healthy for the pond. They crawl around eating organics that fall to the bottom and algae that grows on pond surfaces. You may even want to buy a few snails to seed the pond with. When the water warms up, you frequently will see little globs of jelly hanging onto surfaces inaccessible to the fish. On the sides of the filter for example. These are sacs of snail eggs.

Nutrients & Fertilizer

 Just like a garden, the plants in the pond need food. For the most part they get all the nutrients they need naturally from fish waste and decomposing plant matter. Lilies, however, are recommended to be fed monthly with pond tabs or plant spikes

Essentially there are three main nutrients necessary for vigorous pond plant growth - phosphorus, nitrogen and potash. Normally fish wastes will provide enough of the first two for healthy plant growth but not always.

If your plants (like parrot feathers) are not a deep lush green in warm sunny weather it usually indicates a lack of nutrient, likely nitrogen. Normally a high fish load will provide enough nitrogen in their waste but if you have a lot of plants, there may not be enough for all. Some types can utilize it faster than others and therefore use it up first. What I usually do is toss a couple of Jobe's Spikes in my upper pond to dissolve every few weeks. They have a pretty high nitrogen content (19%) and are relatively cheap. Don't expect to see a quick color recovery though. Water plants *generally* have a very slow uptake of nitrogen and it may take as long as six weeks to see any deepening of the greens.

You can add potash to the pond and it takes very little to treat. The cheapest way is to buy a small bag/box of *muriate of potash* from garden center. Mix a solution of $1/8^{th}$ lb of muriate of potash to 2 quarts of water for each 500 gallons of pond water. Add that weekly throughout the spring and early summer. You can buy premixed potash solution for about $10 a treatment but mixing your own is much cheaper (about a dime for the same treatment dose).

Another (micro)nutrient often lacking is iron. Iron can also be added using another lawn product called Ironite. Be light on adding Ironite though. A cupful for every 500 gallons weekly is plenty during spring and early summer.

Your plants may very well prosper without adding anything to the water so some judgement is called for. Even with a great biological filter you can overwhelm it by putting in too much fertilizer and end up with water discoloring algae bloom. Or cloudy water. Be especially cautious using any fertilizer with phosphorus in it.

Another thing to note is that adding some of the fertilizers, ironite in particular, may cause the water to get cloudy for a few hours, or even a day or do. If it happens, next time cut down on the dosage a little.

Aphids and other Plant Eaters

One last thing about plants and fish. If you have koi you will very likely not be able to grow anything, They eat the tiny shoots as fast as they appear and eat the roots of floating plants. What you will have to do is protect the plants from their incursions. One way to do that is "fence" the pots off.

You can do it by fastening a coarse plastic mesh (say 1" squares or even bigger) around the pot that flares out as it reaches up to the surface. One problem with a fence and lilies is the way it inhibits the spreading of the lily pads across the top of the pond.

A better solution is to fashion a small "globe" of plastic mesh to the top of the lily pot so the pads and flowers can grow up through and spread out.

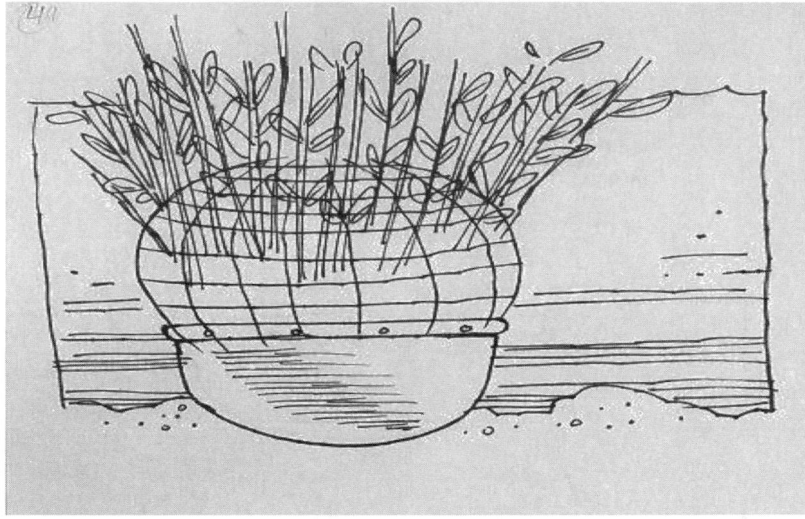

Another idea for floating plants like hyacinth is to take a floating ring (maybe a hula hoop,) and fasten some netting so it hangs down (looks like a crab net) to protect the plant.

 For lilies yet another is enclose the lily root in a large mesh bag with a stone to hold it on the bottom.

And yet another idea is to fasten a plastic grid of large squares (up to 2" square) on top of a container. The illustration below is a 42"L x15"W x 12"Deep tote sitting on bricks. The plants are sagitteria.

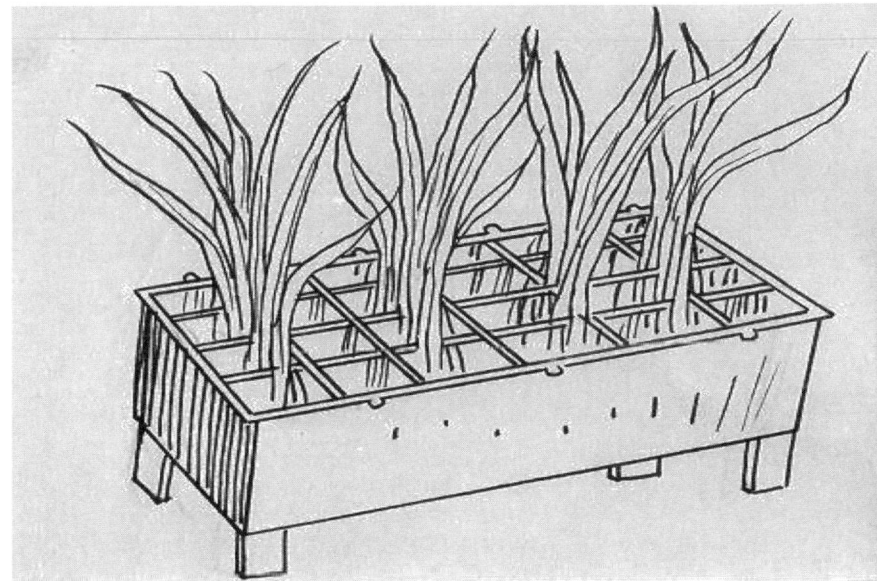

Another trick that can work well is to take a milk crate and fasten some small floats around the top edges and put some floating plants like water hyacinth inside it. The openness of the crate allows plenty water movement around the hanging roots. Small fish will easily swim in and out but the big plant eating lunks won't be able to get at the roots and kill the plants.

n this picture you can see some of the extensive root structure hyacinth develop. They are in a floating milk crate to protect the roots from the koi.

Bugs

You may get an infestation of aphids or other bugs that eat your plants. Obviously you don't want to be spraying a pesticide on them because you could end up poisoning the fish and/or contaminating the water that animals and birds may drink. An effective deterrent to try is mixing a little liquid soap in a spray bottle of vegetable oil. The vegetable oil spray covers the leaves without suffocating them and repels the bugs. The soap is to mix the oil with the water and make it more viscous. You could even try just the vegetable oil alone. It won't harm the pond or its inhabitants. Might just put a little film on the surface for a day or two.

Might even work on the roses. Worth a try. Certainly cheaper and more environmentally sound.

Chapter 7 – Miscellaneous

KEVIN

What's a Kevin? A Kevin is pretty near an absolute requirement for a Ponder (see Glossary). A Kevin is a strong healthy adult (preferably) with whom you have a good relationship. He should be good natured, agreeable and live within easy distance of the pond whenever there needs a waterfall realignment, a hole dug, rocks moved, a pond or stream added, or ...

My Kevin is my son. Yours could be a neighbor, a brother, a sister, a fellow ponder, ... anyone who shares your dreams.

STOCK TANK

Stock tanks can be found, or at least ordered, at Home Depot and/or Livestock/Feed stores. They make very good filter containers.

COLORING DYE

In recent years a new technique has come out to retard algae growth and that is to dye the water, usually a blue tint. While this works pretty well, I think it's best used in a plant only pond as it tints the colors of the fish. The dye has to be renewed on a monthly basis. Dyeing is not something I recommend at all as a general rule, but like most things it does have its place. (Just not at my place.)

EGG CRATE

Reference has been made in several places to "egg crate"". "Egg crate" is a plastic PVC grid of ½ squares. It is often used in florescent lights as a light diffuser. It's not too expensive (around $8 for a 2' X 4' sheet) and is very easy to use to make a dandy grate out of for the bottom of your lava rock filter.

It can be glued if necessary using regular PVC cement. The easiest way I have found to cut egg crate is using a snub nosed electrical wire cutter (called "wire dykes"). Wire dykes are much easier than a saw for cutting pieces to fit in an irregular shape.

You can find egg crate in larger home centers that have a decent electrical department.

AIR LOCK IN FILTER DISCHARGE LINE

If you locate your filter some distance away from the pond and use a length(s) of hose or piping discharging back to the pond, be very careful there are no high spots in the run of pipe (or hose or ...). What can happen, and often does, is the water running down the hose will drag air with it. It has to do with friction and adhesion principles. The air will then accumulate in the high spots, effectively reducing the interior diameter of the pipe cutting the water flow significantly, sometimes to only a trickle.

The same phenomenon will happen to some extent even without a high spot. The flow of the water drags air with it and at some point the pressure of the air trying to escape up the pipe comes in balance with the drag of the water and cuts down on pipe capacity. Over even a short distance it can result in a significant reduction in interior pipe size. Even if the water level rises above discharge hole and no more air can get drawn in, the air that's in there can't get out due to the drag of flowing water.

Remember we are only dealing with gravity and friction induced pressures here, probably tenths or hundredths of a pound, nothing like the head pressure on the discharge side of a pump.

SILICONE CAULKING

Silicone is indispensable to the ponder for making connections, sealing minor leaks, etc. Use it liberally, especially if you make the underwater lights (below). You don't have to buy the most expensive stuff though the couple bucks difference for the tube (and you'll use far less than a tube) is not a big deal. It all works pretty good. Just don't be stingy with it.

UNDERWATER LIGHTS

Underwater lights make an interesting addition to a pond. They are usually expensive to buy (around $200 and up) but not very difficult to make yourself. All you need is a low voltage transformer from an outdoor light setup. They (light setups) are often on sale at Home Centers for under $50. Individual transformers are usually more expensive ($100 and up). Better yet, find one at a garage sale.

You will also need is a small bag of cement, an auto headlight, a soldering iron, a little silicone and you're in business (almost). Get the wattage of the transformer (it should be marked right on it) and go to the auto store and buy headlight(s) wattage that adds up to close to the transformer wattage. The wattage doesn't need to be an exact match but the total wattage of the bulbs used shouldn't exceed the capacity of the transformer. (You can go a little over, say maybe 10% or 20%, but it's better to stay under and you won't have to worry about eventually burning out the transformer.) A large transformer (over 50 watts) is able to support multiple headlights. Headlight wattage can run from as low as 25 watts each.

Wrap the ends of the wire (regular lamp 18 gauge wire is fine) around the terminals on the headlight and solder them fast. (There are usually 3 terminals on the headlight - ground, low beam & high beam. Connect to the ground and the high beam.) Make sure the wire is long enough from wherever you are placing the light to reach back to the transformer in one continuous length. Also make sure there aren't any splices or breaks in the insulation on the wire that could/will "leak" electricity underwater or even above ground. If you do have to splice it, coat the splice liberally with silicone. Let the silicone harden then wrap it with electrical tape.
Fasten the ends of the wires to the transformer and plug it in to make sure it works. If making up several bulbs, do the same for each one. Don't leave any on very long though, the headlights will get very very hot in short order. Liberally coat the bulb terminals and wire ends with a big glob of silicone to prevent water causing a short.

Once the silicone has set (usually a couple hours), mix enough cement to fill the box the headlight came in. Pour the cement in the headlight box about half full or a little more (you will probably have to wrap the box with tape to keep it from bulging and falling apart). Push the headlight down into the wet cement being careful to make sure the wire insulation doesn't touch the bulb. You may want to stick a handle in the cement while you are at it. A short piece of clothesline works well. Tie a small knot in each end and just push an end with a knot in it into the cement on either side of the box leaving a loop for the handle. When the cement dries, you're in the lighting business.

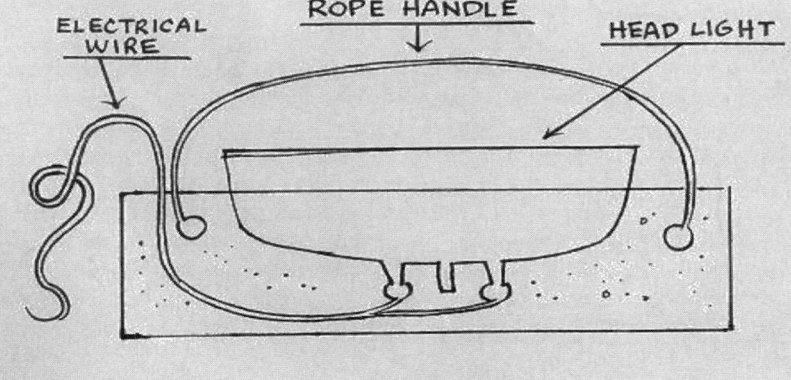

The handle will make it much easier to move the lights around in the pond to get that just right "Berkley Busby" effect. They can be especially attractive shining up into a fountain or waterfall. To get colored lights, try taping or gluing tinted cellophane over the bulbs.

<u>**DO NOT DO NOT DO NOT DO NOT**</u>

<u>plug the lights into anything other than a GFI outlet.</u>

FILTER MATERIALS

For biological filtering the name of the game is surface area where bacteria can grow. While nothing is more cost effective than lava rock in terms of available surface area, many other materials will work well also. The main problem with most other types comes when flushing the material. The bacteria often get washed off and it takes time for them to get reestablished.

The same thing happens with a high flow rate from a large pump. The bacteria either get washed away by the high flow rate or just can't get established to begin with.

For mechanical filtering, synthetic padding, such as a hot air furnace filter, works very well. The problem with furnace filters is that some have a coating that could be toxic to the pond. Make sure you wash them thoroughly before using them the first time. Several of the sources (see References Chapter) sell filter padding that is ideal for ponds. Putting a pad or two on top of the lava rock filter or somewhere in the discharge stream of your filter will go a long way towards "polishing" your water.

Another dandy source of matting is Cobra roofing vent material. It's more coarse than the other padding but it's reasonably cheap ($40 for a 20' long X 10.5" wide roll at Home Depot) and appears to be a lot sturdier that the other matting material I've used. It would be an excellent choice to cover Undergravel Filter pipes.

RAKE

A plastic rake for retrieving stuff that falls in the pond, or removing leaves, etc. that blow in the pond is very handy. Take a child's plastic rake and fasten it to an old broom handle or long pole and you will have a dandy retrieval tool.

BULKHEAD FITTINGS

Bulkhead fittings (for the filter) can be found in marine supply stores. They are long threaded pipe nipples with a wide flange on one end and a wide threaded flange nut. A nylon 1¼" fitting should run about $6. Another source is plumbing supply stores. Several of the catalogs listed in the References Chapter also have a decent selection of bulkhead fittings.

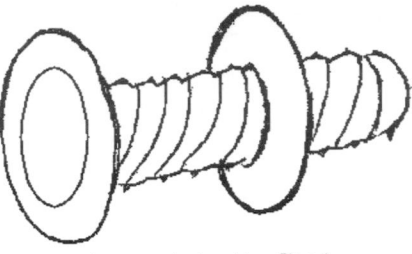

Flanges

"Through hull" fitting

Silicone liberally each facing side of the flanges before tightening. A lot, even most, will squeeze out when the flange gets tightened and can be wiped off with a rag before it sets. This is not a place to get stingy with the silicone, especially if you have made an oversize hole for the fitting.

HOLES for the BULKHEAD FITTINGS

If you don't have a hole saw to make the right size hole for the bulkhead fitting, what you can do is drill as large a hole as you can using a wood bit, then widen the hole with a curved coarse wood rasp. You can get a cheap rasp for a couple bucks in a hardware store. With a little care, you can get a pretty decent fit.

Cutting a perfect hole with a jigsaw is beyond most of us, or me anyway, so if you use one, cut the hole small and use the rasp to get a snug fit.

AUTOMATIC WATER FILLERS

Several of the catalogs advertise Automatic water Fillers for ponds (some under $10). One fella I heard of made one up out of an old toilet bowl filler and float. Whatever works!!!

While a neat idea, there is one drawback to auto fillers if you are using "contaminated" water (chlorinated, for example) water. Because they shut off at a predetermined level, the pond never overflows. If you don't do regular water changes, contaminates can build up in the pond as the water evaporates. Not a problem for most people but something to consider.

BARREL PONDS

If you don't have a place in the yard to put a pond, you might want to consider a Barrel Pond for the porch or patio. Landscape centers sell large half barrels as planters. All you have to do is put in a liner and you're all set. In this case you could probably even get by with using a plastic tarp for a liner. Pick up an undergravel filter plate from an aquarium store, an inch or two of gravel on top, an airstone to draw the water through the gravel and you're in the pond business.

Those half barrels can make a dandy filter container as well. Probably fit into the pond decor a lot better than a plastic barrel too. One fella has several barrels stacked up and arranged so the filter is in the top barrel and overflows into the ones below. A nifty idea but takes some "tuning" to get the overflows right.

BARLEY HAY

An agricultural agency in England has found Barley Hay to be an effective "anti-algae" agent. What happens is that as the hay decomposes, certain bacteria are created that are especially hungry for water discoloring algae. While this is really only relevant to large ponds, if you have access to some hay, it couldn't hurt to drop some in your pond. Try to put it where it will be in the water flow but won't get sucked into the pump strainer. There have been reports of other types of hay working as well but the barley hay is supposed to generate the best natural "algaecide".

SKIMMER (home made)

If you have a lot of leaves falling in your pond, you may want to install a surface skimmer. Pond Supplies of America (see References Chapter) has a nifty setup that combines with a bottom draw intake for the main filter pump. It's very similar to setups used in large underground pools.

I made my own skimmer for those infrequent times there is a lot of floating debris after a wind storm (mostly pine needles).

What I did was take an old plastic wash basin maybe 18" wide, 15" deep and 6" high or thereabouts. I cut a wide hole in a wide side (front) from the top nearly down about an inch from the bottom. I left the rim on for stability and strength. It's wide enough so that there is probably less than 4" left on either side, leaving more than a 12" wide X 5" high opening.

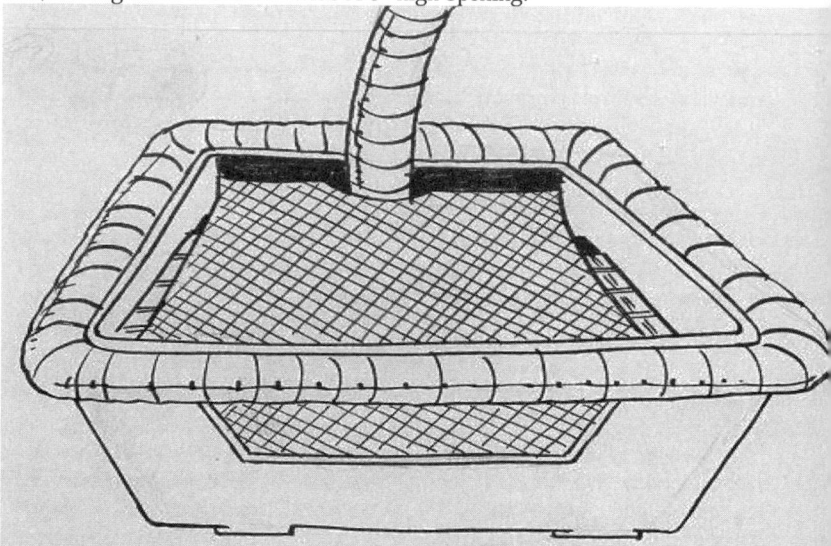

(Front view)

Around the top just under the rim I drilled a series of small holes through which I threaded plastic ties. The ties were used to hold a piece of 1 1/4" pool hose used to keep the basin afloat. The hose goes completely around the top of the basin just under the rim. The ends of the hose are sealed with rags and silicone (what else?), then wrapped with a piece of plastic held in place with wire ties, which keeps water from getting in the hose.

Inside the basin is a small pump (a small power head works nicely) covered with a piece of fiber matting. The pump draws surface water and floating debris through the opening and discharges it out the other side.

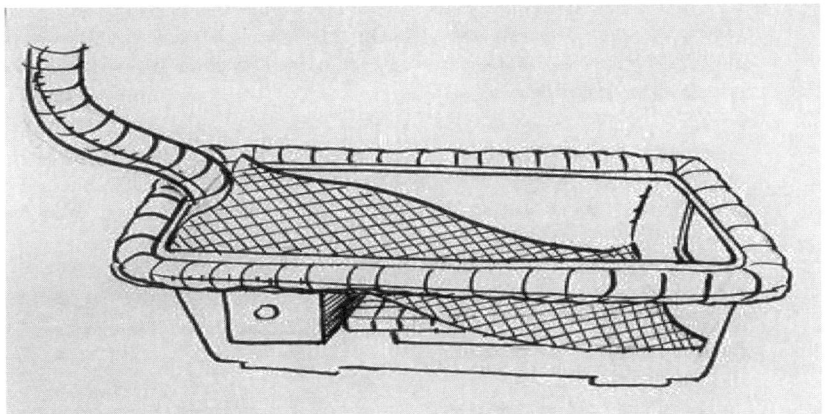

(Cutout view from the side)

The hose coming out the top of the pump is a piece of garden hose. I use a piece of egg crate to increase the draw area of the matting across the entire bottom of the basin rather than just the matting around the pump.

Costs:
1) Basin - couple bucks (actually In Stock).
2) Piece of Pool hose - In Stock (scrap).
3) Piece of garden hose - In Stock (scrap).
4) Plastic ties - In Stock
5) Filter matting - In Stock.
6) Egg Crate - In Stock.
7) Power Head Pump 15-25 bucks (actually In Stock).

That's it. Pretty crude looking but works really well. Since it's only needed once in awhile and then only usually overnight, the ugly appearance doesn't bother me.

ULTRAVIOLET LIGHTS

UV lights are often used in ponds to keep them algae free and from all reports they work can very well (by killing the algae spores as they form). UV lights do have a critical roll, though, in protecting expensive show fish from diseases and parasites.

Drawbacks to UV lights are:

They are relatively expensive (in the $200 neighborhood). There can be a wide price range here.

They have to be "sized" right. That is you can't have too large (or too fast) a flow going past the bulb(s) to be effective. Too small a flow and it won't be effective enough.

The bulbs have to be replaced every year and often every 6 months. That can be extended considerably by using a timer and only running it a few hours a day.

They need clear water to be effective Turbid or dirty water doesn't allow the algae to get exposed to the UV rays.

Plant Soil

For most plants, especially if you have them in pots, mix in some clay (maybe 50% or even more) with the soil or sand you use. Most water plants will do well in a clay base. They clay gives them a good foundation for the roots to hold onto, especially for plants that grow well out of the water (like cattails or iris) in a bog section, for example.

If you don't have any clay easily available you can use a clay based kitty litter. Experiment a little with it first though. Some brands will infiltrate into the water a great deal of "dust" and cloud the water for a few days. Mix your pots up outside the pond and fill them with water to get the dust washed off before putting them in the pond.

FILTER ODORS

If you flush the filter and there is a noticeable odor, then you know you have a problem. The lava rock (or whatever media) has plugged sections that have gone anaerobic because no water is passing by. What you must do then is remove the lava rock and flush all sediment out of the filter. Replace the lava rock. Then flush it more frequently than you have been in the past.

Don't wait for the flow to slow down before flushing the filter. If the flow is slowing down, it means the water passages in the filter media (lava rock) are getting plugged. That means 2 things:

1) There is less water being exposed to bacteria because of plugged passages.

2) Those plugged areas will very likely go *anaerobic* (without oxygen) and kill the existing bacteria. That's where the smell comes from.

If you have made your filter easy flushing (with a large drain hose) you'll save an awful lot of work later on.

LARGE ROCKS

If you have room in the pond (and before you fill it for the last time), you may want to have a section with a large "boulder pile". It could look really neat and especially if you arrange them to have the maximum amount of spaces, even tunnels, between them. The fish will be constantly swimming through and between them.

A good choice is sandstone. The type I used is very light to handle (so light some pieces had to be concreted on the bottom to make them sink) but look very very heavy, even ominous. Just be careful as sandstone can have very sharp edges. Another advantage to sandstone is, again, surface area for bacteria to grow. Not a justification for using sandstone but like Grandma's chicken soup ...

If you do decide to use boulders, it's best to probably not have them against the lining directly. As mentioned before a few inches of gravel makes a dandy padding. Or if you are not using gravel at least put some extra lining pieces under the rocks.

STONE EDGING

If you have used stone edging around the pond, you may want to mortar the stones in place. I'm not recommending it, just a suggestion. It will keep them from moving or getting dislodged. Otherwise a nice touch is to plant ivy or even clover between the stones and let it grow and fill the crevices.

MORE ON PUMPS

Pumps can be a whole book in itself. To keep it simple there are only two types we are interested in here. The first thing is the "gph" (gallon per hour) rating. You can pretty much take it as a tongue in cheek rating. Rather than counting on it being an accurate number, look at it more as a comparison factor between different pumps.

The first type is a submersible pump (like a cellar sump). They generally pump a pretty fair volume, but usually only at a low pressure. New, they can be had for as little as $60 for a 1200 gph pump. They do have a tendency to eventually leak oil which, while certainly not desirable, is not particularly harmful to the fish or plants. It's a light oil that puts a sheen on the water for a day or two but soon evaporates. If you suspect your pump is leaking oil, you can be pretty confident it ain't gonna last much longer. The oil is part of a seal and when it goes, water will soon make its way into and short out the electrical part of the pump.

Cellar sump pumps aren't meant for 24 hour 7 day continual usage months on end. They are designed for intermittent use and as such will often have a short pond service life, say less than a year, though some folks have had very good luck with them. Again it's a price thing, if you find one really cheap (say for $5 or $10 at a garage sale), it's no big deal to have to replace later on down the road.

Beckett makes a fairly sturdy line of submersible pond pumps that are oilless and designed to run 24 hours a day. If you decide to go with a Beckett, I would recommend the 3900 gph model if your pond is over 1,000 gallons.

You'll get great circulation, have plenty filter power, and good volume for your waterfall. Not gonna have a waterfall you say? Wait awhile, next winter you'll figure out how you can stick one in come spring.

The second types are centrifical pumps (like used in swimming pools). They are relatively cheap for the volumes and pressures they deliver (much higher generally than sump pumps). The disadvantage is that they are located out of the pond with a suction pipe into the pond. The suction pipe requires a good size screened draw area otherwise it will plug quickly with debris and/or draw fish into the pump.

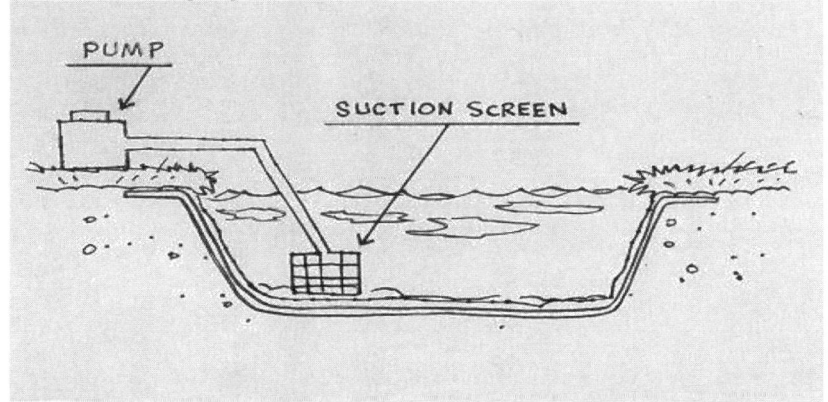

Further they have a tendency to lose the prime (say during a short power outage), run dry and burn up quickly. They require a good deal more plumbing thought during installation to avoid these problems. The general advantages are much greater flow at less electric draw. And they can pump up pretty high (useful for that 40' waterfall you'll want to put in next spring), something most submersibles aren't designed to do.

If you decide to go with a pool pump, make sure you get one with an attached strainer basket that has a check valve built in. They are much easier to prime and stay primed if the pump gets shut off for some reason.

More on Piping Sizing, general water flow characteristics, flow losses, …

Not mission critical stuff here but maybe interesting to the techie types (*It is to me anyway*). Water under pressure flows most efficiently in layers called "laminar flow". The layers usually are very thin, sometimes only a molecule wide. This is a result of friction from flowing along pipe walls. Obviously the smoother the walls, the less friction there is, which is why plastic pipe is such a good water conduit. Iron pipe, even galvanized pipe has far rougher inner surfaces. The rougher the surface, the more flow resistance (friction) there is.

When the water first enters the pipe it is not in laminar flow but "turbulent flow", that is, it hasn't yet been able to form in layers. Laminar flow develops usually within 5 or 6 pipe diameters. Each layer moves at a *slightly* different speed with the slowest near the pipe walls (most friction) and the fastest in the center (least friction). Envision it as a series of ever smaller concentric circles starting at the walls of the pipe.

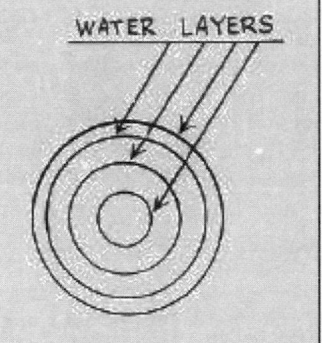

To actually see an example of how friction affects the flow of water, think of any rivers or streams you have seen. They always flow fastest in the center (usually where it's the deepest) and slowest along the banks. It's not the best example of laminar flow but does demonstrate the effect of friction on flow.

Now the flow stays laminar in the pipe until something disrupts it. In the case of ponds, that's usually an elbow or abrupt change of direction causing the flow to go (partially) turbulent again resulting in a pretty fair loss of efficiency. (**The loss can be as high as an additional 10%.**) If you can smooth out the abruptness of a 90 degree elbow with say two 45 degree ells instead then you can reduce the loss pretty significantly, maybe by as much as half. Even more so using 3 30 degree ells.

Think of it the same as highway traffic. It may be moving along at a pretty good clip, but if there is a right turn, it brings traffic to almost a standstill, and it takes a little while to get up to speed after it's completed the turn. Now think of the same traffic making the same turn through a curve in the highway. The larger the curve the faster the traffic can move through it.

Another (additional) way of cutting the losses from pipe friction is to increase pipe size, in effect giving more room to the most efficient inner rings of laminar flow. (Effectively the same as putting more lanes on the highway.) Going from 1" pipe to 1¼" results in a huge savings (gain in efficiency), especially if pumping any distance (say more than 5 or 10'). 1" pipe is only 65% as big as 1¼" pipe and 1¼" pipe is only 70% of 1½.

Even if you start out with a smaller pump, say with a ½ or ¾" discharge, you'll get a lot more water to your filter and/or waterfall using 1¼" pipe than you will with 1". And if you think you might be adding a larger pump someday, you'd be better off piping from the start with 1½ piping.

Fluid dynamics are a neat thing and not fully understood yet, even today. There's a whole lot more to them than what I've gone into here. But you don't have to understand anything about them to be a ponder. It's just another interesting (to some) aspect of ponding. All you have to do is oversize your pipe, stay away from 90 degree ells and you'll be okay.

If you decide to use plastic piping you will likely be better off using black ABS rather than PVC (which is usually white). PVC is easier to work with, has a myriad of fittings that glue easily together and looks pretty good; but it is pretty rigid and does not bend easily. ABS is generally cheaper and can fairly easily be made to bend (especially when heated a little with a hair dryer of some other heat source), often eliminating the need to use any elbows. Heating and bending take a little practice and experimentation, so have some extra pieces on hand.

Bird repellent

In addition to the white gravel and clear water as a bird repellent, you can try one of those realistic plastic owls. It sort of acts like a scarecrow in that it makes birds leery of hanging around. (But they soon enough get used to it.)

Another thing to try if they are a bother is to let some bright yellow plastic (or polyethelene) lines float on top of the water. Stretched across from one side or end of the pond to the other. It inhibits ducks and geese coming in for a landing. If they land outside the pond and walk into the water (wily critters those geese), you might try stringing it along the edges if the pond on a series of sticks about 8 or 10 inches off the ground.

Many home centers carry polyethelene line as clothesline.

Chapter 8 – Summary

Well that's pretty much all you need to know to build and maintain a pond. Don't worry about making mistakes. That's part of the fun. There are only 4 kinds of ponders, those who wish they had done it years before; those who wished they did it differently; those who will do it differently next time; and those who wished they had/hadn't listened to so and so. A true ponder is never satisfied with the status quo.

Just like real estate (location, location, location), enjoyable ponds with *clear* water are Filter, Filter, Aerate!!! (Location is all important too though.) Whether you filter biologically, mechanically; "naturally" (plants, etc.) or some other way, except {shudder} chemically, do your best to aerate the water. I've kinda harped on aeration in the book and I apologize to you for it but I wanted to emphasize how important, even critical, it is. If not with a waterfall, then with surface currents and maximal movement of the water by simply locating the intake of pump as far away from the discharge as possible. Or a fountain. Or ...

Be positively anal about getting the pond level all the way around when digging and setting up. Some real horror stories out there from people who ignored this "rule". Your ground may have an imperceptible slope to it and you don't realize it but believe me you will when you first fill the pond.

Locate a good size section of the pond where it will get at least some sunlight if you can.

And within limits of common sense don't be afraid to experiment. That's half the fun.

COSTS

Let's just take a look at absolute costs. In an early chapter an example was used that was 15' long by 8' wide that would require a liner 20' long x 14' wide. With some judicious shopping around let's say we found one that size for $150.

We decide to go with a big pump and buy a 3900 gph Beckett (my personal favorite) for $150. We find a plastic barrel for $25 at a local chemical company. Fittings run $50 for bulkhead fittings and some plastic pool hoses. 5 cubic feet of lava rock is $30. $100 for white gravel and piping for the undergravel filter pipes. (We won't buy the power head pumps until next year {grin}.) $10 for 100 feeder goldfish.

There we go, there's the necessities for under $500 as I promised at the beginning. (If you noticed I ran a little over, not to worry, I probably paid too much for some stuff. Almost everybody is a better shopper than me.) You'll likely end up going for at least another $500 or so probably before you're finished for fish, rocks, plants, etc. and over time even more. But you've got a good start for under $500 which will give you a million bucks in daydreams. **Not a bad ROI** (Return On Investment).

Before starting the excavation, and even before ordering the liner, sit down and draw it out on paper. Show a couple cross sections from the sides and ends to get an idea of how you want it to look, especially the bottom configuration. Don't forget to order some extra liner if you're planning on a waterfall or a secondary bog pond or ... It doesn't hurt to have some extra laying around anyway. You'll always find a use for it.

After you get the liner in and a few fish and plants started, don't be in a rush to get everything together "just so". It's been my experience, and I've been through the pond process several times, it generally takes a year for a pond to look like, well, a pond. Allow a couple months to let the biological filters get well established (flushing frequently the first few weeks) before loading up on too many fish. Put a couple bucks worth of feeder fish in the second day and then add gradually over the next few weeks/months.

Don't spend too much the first year on exotic fish or plants. Wait until you get some experience under your belt. Mistakes are bound to be made, even with the most slavish attention paid to all the "rules' and "advice" you will get. Just chalk them up to experience.

You can build your pond like is outlined in the book with all the filtering systems or you can build it with no filters in whatever shape, size water or location you want. It's your pond, your creation. All it takes is a little common sense. There are very few rules, other than those you make yourself. I do hope you will at least put some gravel in the bottom though **and don't forget the GFI.**

Tinkering

(Hmmm... What can I do next?)

If you're a true "ponder", you'll be tinkering with it for years, sort of like those wonderful Japanese Gardens we hear so much about. As I said in the beginning, "It should be understood at the outset that if one talks to 100 'Ponders' (Pond aficionados), one will get about 350 ideas on how to best build one, mainly consisting of: 'How I built this one (100)', 'What I wish I had done (100)' & 'My next one is gonna be like (150).' "

Contact the Author

If you have any questions you think I can help you with, I can be reached through email (PondersBible@SwedesDock.com) or write to me in care of the publisher (please include a SASE). I'll respond promptly, I promise. Usually the same day with email.

Glossary of Terms Used

Airstone - A porous "stone" usually made out of a synthetic that is formed around a small pipe. When attached to an air supply, it emits a fine stream of bubbles that expand as they rise in the water column. When used in an enclosed space (like a pipe or tube) the rising expansion creates a suction behind it as it pushes the water upward. This why they can be used in the place of pumps in some applications (our UG filter for example). Airstones in open water are very good are creating a water circulation between the bottom and the surface and not only aerate the water from the surface of the air bubbles, but by causing surface movement, increasing the air/water interaction.

In a pond application, it's best not to use the smallest bubble grade airstone as it will plug far more quickly than a medium or coarse bubble grade. They plug from both the inside (particulates drawn in the pump from the air) and from the outside (when the air is shut off, water fills up the airline and brings particulate with it.)

Aeration - The act of water absorbing oxygen from the air. Water can only absorb oxygen from its surface. That's why I recommended using a spray nozzle when filling the pond. The individual water droplets have infinitely more surface area than a stream of water. It's the reason why moving water is so much more healthier than still water, far far more water gets exposed to the air.

Aficionado – See "ponder".

Algae – The name give almost any form of plant life that forms "spontaneously" in water from a combination of nutrients and sunlight. It ranges from single celled microscopic forms (that turn the water green) to out and out plants (like string or hair algae). There are literally hundreds of distinctly different forms of plants that come under the heading of "algae".

Anaerobic – A condition that occurs when the available oxygen is used up. It normally occurs in still water where there isn't any turnover and the ambient organics decomposing ("oxydizing") use up the available oxygen in the water. Very often the water will have a rotten egg smell.

Automatic Filler – A float switch attached to a water source (usually a garden hose) that opens up if the water level falls below a certain point and closes when the level reaches a certain point.

Automatic Low water Shutoff – A float switch attached to the electric power line of the pump that shuts off if the water level falls below a certain point.

Bacteria - Ubiquitous organisms that form naturally, various types of which are involved in the putrefaction, fermentation and breakdown of organics. In ponds the type we are most interested in convert the ammonia in fish wastes to a form unusable by water discoloring algae.

Channeling - occurs when the lava rock starts to get plugged with detritus and the water forms channels in the rock so that it flows the channels rather just percolating up evenly through all the rock. You can actually see where the water is coming up through the rocks.

Bottom Gook - See Mulm.

Buffer - When talking about ponds, a buffer is an entity that absorbs or moderates rapid environmental insults or changes. For example a larger, a deeper pond provides more of a buffer for rapid temperature changes than a smaller shallow one.

Or in a worst case scenario, if a can of poison falls into a large pond it will be diluted a lot more than in a small one and consequently be less detrimental. In this case the pond might be called a buffer.

A better example would be crushed oyster/clam shells as a pH buffer. If an acid charge gets into the pond (say a ton of oak leaves) the shells will "absorb" the sudden influx of acidic content to some extent raising the low pH. It will do the same for high alkaline influxes as well, drawing down the high pH (to about 8.3).

Glossary

Check Valve - a valve that lets a fluid (air or water) in a pipe go in a single direction. A check valve is often used between the pump and the filter to prevent dirty water from draining (flushing) out of the filter back into the pond when the pump is shut off. I don't recommend one for this use as it usually is only a little dirt and will clear up quickly when the filter restarts. The cost of the check valve doesn't justify the minor irritation. Check valves also restrict the flow of water through them a little (some significantly) and I hate to cut back on efficiency.

A check valve is a good idea on an air stone though. When the air pump shuts down, back pressure from the pond forces dirt into the airstone often causing it to plug up. If the air pump is below the surface level of the pond (usually not a consideration in ponds), the water can siphon back into the air pump, damaging it.

Most above ground centrifugal pumps use a check valve to keep a prime during a pump shutoff.

Decomposition – The natural breakdown of once living organics into nutrients (usually), and toxic poison(sometimes) like ammonia as well.

Egg Crate - A grid made of pvc with ½ squares that comes in sheets 2' X 4'. It's used as a light diffuser in many fluorescent ceiling lights. It costs about $8 a sheet in Home Depot.

Floc –Material excreted by bacteria when it consumes nutrients in water. Roughly analogous to feces.

Fungus - A large group of (micro to large) organisms that live by decomposing and absorbing the organic material in/on which they grow. (Mushrooms and mildew to name a couple familiar ones). In ponds some fungi can literally be "flesh eating" when they reside on fish.

GFI - Ground Fault Interrupt. An electrical term for an especially moisture sensitive electrical outlet. GFI's are mandatory for use in wet or damp environments. It's very dangerous not to use one around a pond. With a submersible pump as it is possible for the pump to develop a short circuit and still keep operating. Touching the water when that happens can cause a severe shock, even death.

GPD, GPH, GPM - Gallons per Day/Hour/Minute. How most pumps are rated, but not to be taken as gospel for what they will actually deliver. Best used as a comparison between pumps.

Head - Another pump measurement, usually expressed as "feet of head". To convert Head to pounds pressure, divide the Head by 2.3. (Head / 2.3 = Pounds pressure capacity of the pump). Many pumps (especially sump pumps) will have a high volume (GPH) but at a low head. That means they can move a lot of water, but the can't push/pull it very high. For example to raise water 5 feet (say for a waterfall), the pump would have to develop 12 feet of head. Volume is significantly cut back as height is increased.

Lava rock - An extraordinarily porous type of rock that has a massive internal surface area where bacteria can grow and act as a biological filter converting ammonia (from fish and plant respiration) into nutrients used by plants but not water discoloring algae.

Limiting Factor - The factor, usually a nutrient, that limits the growth or expansion of a form of life. If a plant requires a combination of nutrients to prosper and one is removed, it doesn't make any difference how much there are of the rest of the nutrients, the form referred to can't grow, In ponds it usually refers to algae growth.

Water discoloring algae can't get generated without phosphorus, nitrogen and sunlight for example. If you have plants that use up all available phosphorus before the algae can get generated then it doesn't make any difference how much sunlight and nitrogen is in the water, the algae can't get started. In this example phosphorus is the limiting factor.

Muck – See Mulm.

Mulm – is decayed and decaying organics on the bottom of the pond, particularly in the Spring after a winter of accumulation. (Decay slows down considerably in colder water.) If you have a gravel bottom (particularly if you have a UG filter under it) you should have very little mulm, if any, to contend with. If you don't have a gravel bottom, it's not necessarily a bad

Glossary

thing to leave in as long as you don't find it unsightly, especially if you have good aeration. It provides healthy "food" for plants and other pond denizens to grow in.

Organics – Once living matter that gets into the pond one way or another. Fish feces, leaves, uneaten fish food, fertilizers from runoff, dead algae, dead fish or snails, … are all organics that decay. The decomposing process (oxydation) is ongoing and continually uses up oxygen.

Oxydation – The process of breaking matter down using oxygen. Oxydation occurs not only in decomposing organics but in inorganics as well. Rusting iron, for example, is a form of oxydation in an inorganic material.

Oxygen Levels - Usually expressed in ppm. As you are well aware, almost every living thing uses oxygen. Plants, fish, bacteria, even the decomposition process. When there is so little oxygen (5-8 ppm) in water to start with, it's important to keep replenishing oxygen to the pond, hence my constant harping on aeration.

For example the maximum saturation of oxygen in pond water will be somewhere around 9 or 10 ppm (depending on ideal conditions, temperature, etc.). Pond life will stay pretty healthy as long as the oxygen level stays above 5 ppm but most will get stressed below that. As you can see there's a very narrow range. To put it into perspective, the "fluid" we live in (air) runs about 230,000 ppm of oxygen.

PONDER - Pond aficionado. Proper term for whom owning a pond is more than just an acquisition, it's an obsession. The pond is NEVER perfect to a true ponder. It always will need ...

Power Head - A small pump used in aquariums. They range in size from 150 gph to as high as 500 gph, costing from $15 to $50.

PPM - Parts Per Million. A relative measuring term. An oxygen content of 5 ppm means that for each million parts of water, five parts are oxygen.

UG - Under-Gravel filter. A holey pipe under the gravel through which water is drawn for supplemental filtration.

Zone (1-10) - A planting guide put out by the US Department of Agriculture of normal and expected low temperatures in areas of the country. Generally Zones 1 & 2 (coldest) are in Alaska and Canada. Zones 9 & 10 (warmest) are found only in the southernmost tips of the USA.

References & Sources

The Internet is a wonderful resource for ponders. Just do a search for "ponds" with almost any search program and you'll come up with hundreds of references (hopefully mine will be near the top!!!). Lotsa folks have built their own ponds, are justifiably proud of them and like to show them off. Plenty of pictures, how-to diagrams, tips and instructions. (*Caution though, while all advice is good intentioned, not all is good. Common sense needs to be applied when "surfing" pond sites.*)

Most of this chapter is a reproduction of Swede's Pond Links on the Internet (**http://www.SwedesDock.com/PondLink.sht**). There are quite a few "real" addresses and phone numbers here as well for you "non netters" as well though.

Links to my own pages first (naturally):

http://www.SwedesDock.com/Pond.sht - Building a Pond - Great for first timers and new Ponders. "A wonderful read" {he said modestly}.

http://www.SwedesDock.com/Pondltrs.sht - Pond Questions - Where you just might find an answer to your question.

http://www.SwedesDock.com/Ponideal.sht - MY Ideal Pond - (*Dream on Fool*)

http://www.SwedesDock.com/pondstrw.sht - Using Straw to control Algae.

http://www.SwedesDock.com/Pondpics.sht - Pictures of my pond and others.

http://www.SwedesDock.com/Pond0997.sht - An end of season report on my pond for 1997

http://www.SwedesDock.com/Pond1998.sht - Instructions to build: a simple skimmer, plus thoughts on Airborne algae and salt.

http://www.SwedesDock.com/Pondlgfl.sht - Dusty's big filter (for a 15,000 gallon pond).

http://www.SwedesDock.com/Pondnutr.sht - Managing Nutrients to Control Algae. A dandy article on nutrients and how they affect clear water. (Note - this originally appeared in an issue of Pam's Puddle. It was so good I contacted the author and he consented to putting a copy up here.)

http://www.SwedesDock.com/pondfold.sht - Frogs, Fish, Flora, Fauna and Filter Folderol. More stuff on stuff.

Various Pond links

I have broken the rest of the links into Sections:

1) Personal Pond Sites - mostly put up by hobbyists like me.

2) Large Pond Sites for those interested in either growing fish commercially or having acreage size ponds.

3) Technical Sites - that go into pH, water quality, nutrients, disease and the like as well as mechanical how to do it yourself stuff.

4) Commercial Sites where to buy plants, liners, pumps, etc.

Again I remind you that I have visited each of the following and found it worthwhile unless noted otherwise. I am not trying to have the world's largest collection of links, only good quality ones. If you know of any yourself, send them along and I'll post them should they meet my rigid, completely subjective, ever changing and reputedly whimsical criteria.

Personal Pond Sites

http://www.charm.net/%7Ehuribead/ponders.html - Ponder's Places. A collection of different Pond Pictures. Nice visit. You can spend an easy hour here.

http://www.geocities.com/RainForest/Canopy/1104/pond.html -An Urban Oasis. Just a nice place to visit. Hosted by Wynnie the Dog.

http://www.geocities.com/RainForest/Vines/1648/landscp.html -Bart's water Garden. A very nice job. Friendly and easy on the eyes. Lotsa pictures..

http://www.gl.umbc.edu/~rrhudy1/pond.htm - Robin's Pond. Lotsa good stuff. A rich site with good (well not all is good, a lot seems recycled and not personal experience) info on fish and plants. Check out her "mistakes" page. A real "What Not to Do..." with "professionals".

http://www.geocities.com/PicketFence/Street/1229/ - Trey and Jacque's Pond Page. A very nice setup. Check out their dandy filter housing.

http://members.aol.com/chilemike1/index.html - Mike & Lori's Pond. A really nice looking pond. Might take a little while to load but worth the wait.

http://www.dallas.net/~crush/tips.html - Chuck's Building Tips. An absolute MUST VISIT if you haven't started your pond yet or are contemplating a new one. (*If you need more details than I give, that is. Dunno why you would. {grin}*)

http://www.geocities.com/Heartland/Woods/3088/ - Oakbrook Koi. Absolutely the most work for the least result I have ever seen. A textbook example of how not to build a pond and filters using a textbook(s) and money.

http://www.urban.ne.jp/home/koistaff/eindex.html - Koi Staff. A Japanese site that gives a little history of koi and many pictures (some 30" koi). These are Koi Experts. There is a very good page on disease but the English is difficult to follow (a million times better than my Japanese though, sumi ma sen).

http://www.geocities.com/Heartland/Hills/9613/frmain.html - Lee's Koi Korner. (Maylasian Pond) A Koi enthusiast. Has PLENTY koi links and pictures.

http://www.supernet.net/~suztay/ponds.html - Suzette's Pond. Dandy installation directions for a small simple backyard pond. Dandy Pictures too.

http://www.netdepot.com/~afarmer/Ppage.html - Alan Farmer's Pond Page. Great pictures. Good visit.

http://lafourche.k12.la.us/teymard/pond/ - Terry Eymard's Pond Page. A simple uncomplicated above ground installation. Looks really nice too.

http://www.geocities.com/Heartland/Prairie/8184/pond_index.html - Diary of a First Time Ponder. A very good read.

http://www.geocities.com/Heartland/Hills/9613/frmain.html - Lee's Koi Corner. Some decent discussion and good links.

Http://reality.sgi.com./employees/peteo/index.html - Pete's Pond Page. A neat site, well put together, with a MUCH more elaborate setup than what's talked about here (though *I think* he's lacking on filtration {grin}) .

http://www.h2olily.com/ - Home Page for International lily Society. Just as the title indicates.

http://www.icanect.net/aqualit/page4.htm - Some nifty looking fountains.

http://www.viagrafix.com/pingle/ - Pam's Puddle. Periodic Pond Ezine. Lotsa pond chat, a touchy feely kind of place. Well Worth a visit. Often has good articles.

http://www.gl.umbc.edu/~rrhudy1/pond.htm#problems - Robyn's Pond Page. A horror Story.

http://www.bangladesh.net/~sgray/austin.pond.society/tour96p1.html - The Austin Pond Society. Some neat pond pictures. (Hey, some of their ponds cost more than my house).

http://w3.one.net/~rzutt/alink.html#personal - Lots More Links Caution, Many don't work!!!

(Dusty's recco) **http://www.gardenweb.com/forums/ponds/** - Garden Web Pond Forum.

(Dusty's recco) - **http://www.gardenweb.com/forums/** - The Garden Web Forums. All wonderful

(Dusty's recco) - **http://www.photovault.com/index.html** - Real Eye Candy. (PHOTOS!!) (Note - While not specifically about Ponds, I left it in because there COULD be stuff about Ponds here. {grin})

(Dusty's recco) - **http://www.virtualhomesite.com/landscape/bus.htm** - Worthwhile too(Note - A list of links to all kinds of pond, gardening, farming and ranch supply sites.)

(Dusty's recco) - **http://soli.inav.net/~bickal/pond.htm** - This is a REAL nice SITE!!! 5* Stuff

(Dusty's recco) - **http://cafe.scranton.com/~cww/seedlinks.htm** - Great Site for Stuff! (Note - A list of links to all kinds of gardening stuff mostly)

(Dusty's recco) - **http://landru.i-link-2.net/dusty** - Dusty's Delights. Dusty's home page .

Large Pond Sites

http://home.iSTAR.ca/~ogrady/ - THE BIG PONDER This guy'll REALLY make you jealous. He's in the Big Leagues.

http://ohioline.ag.ohio-state.edu/b374/index.html - Ohio Pond Management Bulletin 374. Ohio State University Extension Service bulletin on Small Pond Management (Big Ponds to us {grin})

http://www.h-mconsulting.com/byaqua.htm A good primer on raising game and food fish in a small pond (1 acre area). Your own private fishing hole per se.

Technical Sites

http://www.SwedesDock/pondpara.sht - A paper on Parasites. I recco highly. Worth printing out. (note - This is a "mirror" I provided because the original link went bad.. It's that good! It also has instructions for making your own hydrometer to test the salinity of your pond.)

http://web2.airmail.net/manteyk/ - Under Lighting - I Tried this and it works GREAT. Only I used a 25watt transformer (in stock) and a 35watt headlight ($7).

http://www.scapes.com/science/index.html - Science in the Pond Good papers on Fish Pain, Quarantine, pH, and more. Dean Earlix, Ph. D. In Pond Biology

http://www.scapes.com/science/phtheory.html - An EXCELLENT article on PH values (probably more than what most of us need to know but if you're having problems ... part of Science in the Pond)

http://falcon.jmu.edu/~jenninms/apps/picsaver/ - PicSaver - is a FREE screen saver that uses your own files to display on the screen. What I did was set up a Folder (directory to you old DOS horses) called Screen Saver Pictures (you can call it anything) and copied my pond pictures to it.

Lately what I've been doing is whenever I run across a neat pond picture on the Net I save it to my hard disk in the Screen Saver folder. It's really easy to do. In Netscape, just point to the picture with the mouse, right click, choose Save As, navigate to the Screen Saver folder, click Okay and that's all there is to it. (Note- Save them to a temporary folder first and try them out there before putting them into your Screen Saver Folder. Many images are in a JPG compressed format PicSaver can't handle. I had to "resave" in uncompressed format to get PicSaver to display them. Email me for more details.)

Now whenever my screen is idle for 3 minutes I'm treated to pond pictures. Fixated? Me? Naw.... {grin}

http://tor-pw1.netcom.ca/~dbrought/pond/maintenance.html#gena
Rec.Ponds.Faq - Frequently Asked Questions on Pond Maintenance. *(Note the address is all one word, including the first dash.)*

http://aquatic-eco.com/techtalk/tt/techtalk_toc.htm - Tech Talk at Aquatic Eco Systems. Lotsa good stuff. A rich site but not pond specific. Lotsa aquaculture info. Well worth a visit.

http://www.saj.usace.army.mil/conops/apc/weed_bio.html - Biological Control of Exotic Aquatic and Wetland Plants. Maintained by the Army Corps of Engineers. You'll be amazed how many plants we buy and grow are actually considered noxious weeds in some areas of the country and world.

http://soli.inav.net/~bickal/deicer.htm - Greg's Pond De-icer. Here's an untried (by me) homemade pond heater. Look around here, some good tips. This site is worth your time, at least it was well worth mine.

http://www.koiusa.com/library/salt.htm A good discussion of the necessity of salt in ponds.

http://www.koiusa.com/library/salt3.htm More on Salt including a home made hydrometer water ($15)

http://www.koiusa.com/question.shtml - KOI USA questions page. If you wanna make yourself crazy with filter information and/or are interested in pond chemistry, look around here.

http://www.webdirectory.com/Science/Oceanography/Aquariums/Pond_and _Goldfish/
- Environmental Organization WebDirectory - *(Note - all one word again)* Science: Oceanography: Aquariums: Pond and Goldfish. Another good place to nose around.

http://www.gdnctr.com/hpond2.htm - What NOT to do by John Shelley. Common sense stuff.

(Dusty's recco) - **http://www.koivet.com/** - Fish Vet great site.

(Dusty's recco) - http://www.aa.net/~koi/encyclo/encyclo.html - Talking koi encyclopedia.

(Dusty's recco) - **http://www.applink.net/cpollard/petfish.htm** - Aquarium Fish Info. Links for those with aquariums and related subjects.

(Dusty's recco) - **http://www.vcnet.com/koi_net/H2Oquality.html** - Pond water Chemistry - A valuable site. Papers on the various elements making up the Chemistry of Pond . For the technoids.

Commercial Sites & Catalogs

http://www.flash.net/~txpphou/ - The Water Plant Stand and Water Edge Basket. Where you can get wire plant stands. Photos & price list online.

http://www.paradisewatergardens.com/ Paradise Water Gardens Lilies & Lotuses. Free catalog 1-800-955-0161

Jermack Cultivated Plants - Free catalog 1-800-226-7759

http://www.greenandhagstrom.com/ Green & Hagstrom. Plant fertilizer and other pond supplies.

OASE PUMPS - Bio filters 1-800-365-3880

http://www.aquatic-creations.com/ Aquatic Creations Ltd. Yet another filter supplier with price lists.

http://www.watergarden.com/ The Water Garden - Indoor and Outdoor Fountains

http://www.marylandaquatic.com/ Maryland Aquatic Nurseries - Free catalog 1-410-557-7615

http://www. michaelgordonltd.com Michael Gordon Ltd - Fountains, statues and stuff.
1-800-928-4886

Pond Gard Liners - advertised as low as .40 per square foot delivered in full rolls
1-419-825-1438

Nycon Products - Plant Feeder Holders & other pond stuff. 1-800-9266

http://www.rainbow-lifegard.com Life Gard Ultraviolet Sterilizers - all kinds of filters and other stuff. 1-800-628-8771

Aqua Ultraviolet - UV filters 1-800-693-4533

Escort Lighting - Exotic garden lighting 1-800-856-7948

Springdale Aquatic Supply & Nursery 1-800-987-5459

Diamond Pumps - for fountains, ponds, plus other pond supplies 1-800-375-3171

AgriTab - Fertilizer Tabs, Spikes & Granules 1-800-398-3803

http://www.aquariumpharm.com/ Aquarium Pharmaceuticals -Fish medications, food, water treatments. 1-800-847-0659

http://www.ultraclear.com/ Ultra Clear - Pond chemicals for clarity, parasites, disease, etc.

Water Garden Gems   Bubble Bead Filters - all sizes 1-800-682-6098

Blue Ridge Fish Hatchery - Quality Fish food 1-800-334-5257

Crystal Palace Perennials - Unusual & High Quality waterplants - free catalog 1-219-374-3419

Kichler Landscape Lighting - Floating pond lights catalog (#k-1589) 1-800-659-8000

http://www.daviscreek.com Davis Creek Nursery - Plants - free catalog

1-800-493-8968

http://energysavers.esuweb.com/esuweb/html/P_HP.htm - Pond Life All manner of pond supplies.

http://www.wickleinaquatics.com/ Wicklein's Water Gardens - Plant & Aquatics nursery
1-800-382-6716

http://www.falling-waters.com/ - Falling Waters - The koi and pond discount store!

Charleston Aquatic Nurseries - Catalog 1-800-566-3264

Laguna - Pond & Water supplies, filters, etc. - Catalog 1-800-225-2700

http://208.234.24.111/pages/yourpond.html - The Water Garden A nice commercial site with plenty pond pictures.

http://www.awebplace.com/theplantplace/toc.htm - The Plant Place. Reasonably priced Fish Food. Not as cheap as Friskies cat food though. {grin} Worth a look around.

http://www.pondshop.com/catalog/koi.htm - Koi by the box - If you want to buy fish in QUANTITY.

http://www.daydreamergardens.com/index.htm Water - Day Dreamers - A commercial site that sells a large selection of plants and has a very nice section of articles on waterfall Building, filtration (beware of poor advice regarding algae here though), etc.

http://www.fishlinkcentral.com - Fish Link Central .The most comprehensive set of Pond links I have found (other than my own {grin}). This site has links to just about anything that swims. I well recommend it.

http://www.metzerfarms.com/ - The Duck Farm If you wanna buy ducks for your pond, check this place out. Worth a trip anyway.

http://www.jbic.com/lilyblooms/hdylily.htm water - Hardy water Lilies Nymphaea) Large selection and reasonable prices. Ask about liner prices. Supposed to have great deals. Free catalog.

http://www.customfountains.com/ - Fountains Galore 'Nuff said.

http://www.shopsite.com/plants/ - More water Plants (This was reccoed by a reader) Nice pics, good variety. Can order Lotus here.

http://www.pacificcoast.net/~ponds/catalog.htm - Discount Pumps & Liners Liner prices look a little high but not too far out of line. *Complete price catalog online so you can get an idea on liner prices.* Plenty other stuff too.

http://www.pondauthority.com - The Pond Authority I visited but found it slow loading. Looks like a complete place to shop. Dunno about service or prices. Haven't bought anything (yet). I listed it because they asked me to and they are in Swedesboro, NJ. How could I resist?

(Dusty's recco) - **http://www.shopsite.com/plants/aisle33.html** - Bog Plants

(Dusty's recco) - **http://w3.one.net/~rzutt/newsletter.html** New Mag. Internet Ponder

(Dusty's recco) - **http://www.clearcatch.com/** - An Invisible Fish Net. They sell a net that's invisible in the water that's supposed to make catching the little critters a snap.

(Dusty's recco) - **http://aquat1.ifas.ufl.edu/** Aquatic Plants

(Dusty's recco) - **http://www.eagle.ca/~wtrgdn/** Burns water Gardens

Phone Resources & Catalogs

<u>Anjon Products</u> - 800-553-5605 - Dusty says they sell 20 to 50 foot wide liners. (**http://www.anjonproducts.com/Pondliners.htm**)

<u>Aquatic Eco-Systems</u> - If you're going to the Big Leagues call 800-422-3939 for a catalog or 407-886-3939. They handle BIG equipment and looks to be an excellent source for the type of stuff for really big ponds. They have a DANDY catalog, well worth the phone call even if you never buy anything.

<u>Zett's Fish Farm and Hatcheries</u> - Also if you're going to the Big Leagues call 814-345-5357 for a catalog. An excellent source for the type of stuff for really big ponds. They sell game fish, daphnia, all manner of plants (*Great prices), and have a dandy catalog. Well worth the price of a phone call. Delivery is a little iffy with Zetts. They don't take credit cards and have an old fashioned accounting system so make sure to save your receipts to check against delivery.

<u>That Fish Place</u> - 800-733-3829 and ask for a Catalog. I buy lotsa stuff there for my pond and my salt water setup. Best prices around for much hardware. (http://www.ThatPetPlace.com)

<u>Pond Supplies of America</u> - 888-742-5772 - Ask for a catalog. They got lotsa good stuff and the prices don't look bad either. (They have a dandy skimmer bottom draw combination setup.) Chris likes to talk ponds.

<u>Bend Tarp & Liner, Inc</u> - **http://www.empnet.com/bendtarp/** - "We are fabricators of PPL-24 liners. I noticed one of your writers found us, (1996) and you were not familiar with our products. We supply our liners for .33 cents a square foot, F.O.B. Bend, OR. Our liners are in fact superior to 40 mil HDPE in strength, and the UV resistance surpasses that of PVC liners. Please take a moment to look at our web page and spec sheet on this product, and your writers will have a new link to quality, fish safe, affordable liners. I really enjoyed your page.
Jan Elliott 800-280-0712"

<u>S P Sheet Metal</u> - 732-929-8666 - They will make a stainless steel custom designed (by you) filter housing. Call for prices. They made one for me and it's a beauty.

References & Sources

BOOKS

There are (quite) a few books on ponds out there, some better than others. Most are, I feel, too darn technical, I mean we're not talking about building the Hoover Dam here. Anyway most all of them have *something* to offer though, something that will spark ideas or perhaps make thing clearer. Here are a few books I thought were halfway decent:

How to Build Ponds and Waterfalls by Jeffery Reid ISBN 1-56465-1959

The Pond Doctor by Helen Nash ISBN 0-80690-6871

Step by Step Ponds, Pools and Rockeries by Penny Swift and Janek Symanowski
ISBN 1-853638-5399

The Complete Pond Builder by Helen Nash ISBN 0-80693-8676

How to Build Ponds and Waterfalls and Much More - The Complete Guide water by Jeffery Reid ISBN 1-5765-195-9

Quick Guide to Pond & Fountains - Step by Step Installation Techniques
ISBN 1-880029-29-4

Gardens by Peter Stadelmann ISBN 0-8120-4928 1

An Owner's Guide to the Garden Pond by Roseanne D. Conrad ISBN 0-87605-447-5

The Garden Pond - by Roseanne Conrad, publisher of Pondkeeper Magazine - a trade magazine.
1-814-695-4325 (to order) $12.95
Earth Ponds – Pond books & Videos from Countryman Press
1-888-494-3197

Index

Index

163

Index

The Ponder's Bible

Book Order Blank

FAX ORDERS – (732) 830-8118. Send this form
TELEPHONE ORDERS – Call 1-877-409-0508 (toll free)
EMAIL ORDERS – Orders@PondersBible.com
POSTAL ORDERS – Carolelle Publishing
        Suite 214
        12 Trenton Avenue
        Lavallette, NJ 08735

Number   **Title**   (Prices are in US dollars)
_____ The Ponder's Bible (B&W) @14.95 | _____
_____ The Ponder's Bible (Color) @26.95 | _____
_____ Shipping**   @ ____ | _____
_____ Additional books**   @ ____ | _____
                      Total | _____

***Shipping US ($4.00 first book, $2.00 each additional). International
(Estimated $9 first book, $5.00 each additional, Note – order will only be
charged for actual shipping costs over US charges.)*

         (Please Print clearly)
Name _____

Address _____

Address _____

City _____State _____ Zip _ _____

Country_____

Payment: ___Check
Credit card: _ Visa __Mastercard _ Optima __AMEX __Discover
_____ __Other
Card number __ __ __ __ - __ __ __ __ - __ __ __ __   Expiration __ __ / __ __
Signature

Book Order Blank

FAX ORDERS – (732) 830-8118. **Send this form**
TELEPHONE ORDERS – Call 1-877-409-0508 (toll free)
EMAIL ORDERS – Orders@PondersBible.com
POSTAL ORDERS – Carolelle Publishing
    Suite 214
    12 Trenton Avenue
    Lavallette, NJ 08735

Number Title   (Prices are in US dollars)
_____ The Ponder's Bible (B&W) @14.95 | _____
_____ The Ponder's Bible (Color) @26.95 | _____
_____ Shipping **   @ ____ | _____
_____ Additional books ** @ ____ | _____
          Total | _____

***Shipping US ($4.00 first book, $2.00 each additional). International
(Estimated $9 first book, $5.00 each additional, Note – order will only be
charged for actual shipping costs over US charges.)*

    (Please Print clearly)
Name _____

Address _____

Address _____

City _____ _____State _____ Zip _____

Country_____

Payment: ___Check
Credit card: __Visa __Mastercard __Optima __AMEX __Discover
_____Other
Card number __ __ __ __ - __ __ __ __ - __ __ __ __ Expiration __ __ / __ __
Signature